Finding Zen in Rebound Dogs

By The Author

THE MAN FROM MYSTERY HILL
a.k.a. THE SOUL COLLECTOR

RESTITUTION

THE PROTEUS CURE
with F. Paul Wilson

THE COLLECTION AND OTHER DARK TALES

MY NAME IS MARNIE

MISSING

THE RAINBOX

JUST STORIES

FINDING ZEN IN REBOUND DOGS

Finding Zen
in Rebound Dogs

A single mom's guide to love and happiness

Tracy L. Carbone

SHADOWRIDGE PRESS

FINDING ZEN IN REBOUND DOGS
First published January 2019
by Shadowridge Press

This work has previously appeared
in a series of blogs as *Rebound Dogs and My New Life*.
It has been revised by the author for this edition.

Book design by Robert Barr, inspiration
provided by James Thurber.

Dog doodles by Tracy L. Carbone.

ISBN: 978-1-946808-13-4

shadowridgepress.com

Acknowledgments

For every life turn I've taken, or not taken, there have been people around me who have made a difference. From romantic partners to family and friends, every person I have come across, no matter how big or small their involvements, contributed to my experiences. Some were terrible, others wonderful, but from all of them, I learned and grew, and became a better person.

I would like to thank everyone I've ever crossed paths with, because if not for our meeting, I would be somewhere else living a different life.

To the real life

Ivy

and

Ryan

who make this a more beautiful world.

Finding
Zen
in Rebound Dogs

Foreword

In July 2011, I was just ending, quite abruptly, an eight month relationship. This guy was great on paper. He was relatively attractive, played guitar, had long-term friends, and a nice family, a house, a good job. He had a crazy ex-wife, which certainly wasn't his fault—we all make mistakes right? Of course if you looked too close at that paper, he had some big issues. But when you're in love, who spends time examining the details? Well, certainly not me. Not then. I was a master at ignoring flags and that time was no different. Within a week or two of living together, the façade faded away and I was left with the real guy.

In his defense, this was not the first time it had happened to me. I painted everyone with a romantic brush and ignored shortcomings or incompatibility even when they were right in front of me.

I asked him to move out, and gave him a week. This was generous since we had been cohabitating only a short time and I felt, at that point in the relationship, and at my age, every suitor has a probationary period. Less than a year was fair game. While I waited for that week to pass, I started this blog in secret. I dashed off to Starbucks with my laptop. I felt utterly sneaky, but also excited. I was going to stop this relationship foolishness once and for all. And I was going to write a blog all about it. It had to be anonymous. And so began the story of Carly G. and Rebound Dogs. I had no idea then that the story of the cynical single mother would turn into a love story with a true happily-ever-after ending.

Except for making myself slightly younger, omitting the presence of my existing Schnauzer, and replacing my old female Siamese cat with a male black cat Henry, a cat I owned briefly some years before, all is true and the same, except for the names. Minor grammar and spelling errors have been corrected, and a few tweaks to the formatting to make it book friendly. Apart from that, all entries are exactly as they were written in the *www.rebounddogs.com* blog which continues the story.

Rebound Dogs and My New Life: Day One

July 29, 2011

A pattern I've had since my first heart-wrenching breakup at sixteen is to start dating again way too soon after swearing never to love again. And to eat too much. Today, that cycle stops. I'm forty-two years old and have been slightly overweight all my life. And slightly overweight would be GREAT but I'm a bit more than that. I want to tie my shoes without hitting a shelf of what I can't honestly still call my baby weight from my fifteen-year-old daughter (from my first failed marriage), Ivy.

I just had a break up (hard to say who started it but I ended it) and it's too soon to write about it publicly less it SOUND! LIKE! AN! ATTACK! And honestly, I think I'm losing my passion for this idea of love. It's starting to not even bother me. I'm becoming too efficient at breaking up with men who lie, change dramatically once we get serious, exhibit mental illness they hid at the onset. I used to cling to unhealthy men and dysfunctional relationships for years, no matter what they did. Those blogs I'll save for another day. Now it's more "been there, done that, here's your hat, what's your hurry."

I run when I hear, "I can change; you're overreacting" or one of my all-time favorites, "If I'd told you that at the beginning you never would have dated me." Nice.

So with this recent breakup which will hurt later once my anger dissipates—when I look back and remember all the good stuff and lament, over hot-from-the-oven brownies, what could have been if, only if—that I might try a new tack. I'm going to get a Rebound Dog.

Forget the siren calls of *Match.com* and *e-harmony* (met the craziest guy ever with their guidance) with their free sign up weekends and their "just about everyone you know met on OUR site!" claims. I am going to stay away from dating until my high school sophomore is in college. At least that's my plan.

I'm going to work hard at my fulfilling yet unremarkable day job, raise my daughter, get a dog who will love me unconditionally and will not go insane. And if he does, I can at least demand a refund. That is not the case, if you were wondering, with the dating sites. I tried. They e-laughed at me.

And I'm going to lose weight. Not to slim up for a man, or to look all snazzy in a slinky cocktail dress, or even so I can shop in the regular woman section and not the "big girl" area. It's for me. And for Ivy, because who can look up to a mother who has a muffin top at her waistband? And for my new dog.

So today is Day One of my new life. I hope you follow my quest to find a Rebound Dog, to lose weight, and to find inner happiness.

Rebound Dogs and My New Life: Day Two

July 30, 2011

Let me start by saying I'm not as overweight as I thought yesterday. Perspective is everything. I broke down and delved into "that part" of my closet where my bigger clothes reside. They're not MUCH bigger, just a little. My MUCH bigger stuff I donated years ago. I also have my "Post Divorce" section. That holds the tiny outfits I could only wear for about six months till the shock wore off and I started eating real food again with reckless abandon.

So I put on a pair of the jeans from the right side of the closet because Friday is Jeans Day in my office, and I felt much better immediately. Also I didn't get lines on my tummy. I decided to stick to my standard diet I always fall back on. I had a Dunkin Donuts Turkey Sausage Flatbread sandwich which was healthy, but then a medium hot coffee with cream—not healthy. Oh well, it all balances out. Smart Ones Mac and Cheese for lunch, and chicken and diet Mac and Cheese for dinner. I'm somewhat of a cheese fiend which is always my downfall. Years ago I lost sixty pounds on the Atkins Diet eating nothing but cheese and meat, but even contemplating that now makes me queasy. And yes, I KNOW it's not about dieting it's about changing your lifestyle, but I need a jump-start.

My daughter is excited about the idea of a dog. Today I checked some breeds online. My aunt has a Tea-Cup Yorkie. She's tiny and Ivy loves her but a dog that small makes me nervous, like I might roll over on her in my sleep and crush her. And yes, my dog will sleep with me.

Since I've made a bad habit of rushing into people relationships I'm going to make sure I take my time to find just the right dog. Tomorrow I'm going to the local animal shelter, just to look. I promise. I WILL NOT COME HOME WITH A DOG.

Wish me luck. Here's to getting it right this time.

Day Three-
And Still Dog-Free
July 31, 2011

This morning I took Henry, my obese black cat, to the vet for his annual check up. Henry's great, getting a little slow as he ages, but he doesn't fill my yearning for a dog. While waiting for him to be called in, I noticed a young couple with an elderly black lab. Both the man and woman had tears in their eyes so it was obvious why they were there. Eventually they were called into the examination room. A few minutes later the humans emerged, crying, without their dog. I could relate because I put my old dog down about ten years ago. Same vet. It started my day on a sad note.

Henry was fine by the way, and the vet, still surely saddened by her last patient's outcome didn't even give me flack about Henry's weight. Once I took my cat home, I hugged him hard, and then rushed out to drown myself in puppies.

Ivy is visiting with her dad's family for a week in San Diego, which to me feels like the other side of the world. I can't imagine anyone living in California after spending a life in beautiful cozy New England but who am I to judge? I miss her, and with the heartbreaking events at the vet, I needed some puppy time.

I stopped by a local puppy store which specializes in mixed designer breeds: YorkiePoos, Morkies, Chi-Poos, and lots of others with combo names I can't remember. I walked in and the clerk said to put hand sanitizer on and go sit on the floor. I did and about a dozen puppies jumped all over me. It was intoxicating. This is the canine adoption equivalent of Speed Dating I bet, not that I've tried that. By the end of the meet and greet session I came dangerously close to bringing home the little Chi-Poo, who looked like a mix of Chocolate Lab, Dachshund and Poodle.

I refrained, reminding myself that this time I'd vowed to take it slow, and that anyone can be super charming for ten minutes. Also, since Ivy hasn't had a say in my past relationships, I figured she needs to be there to help choose the next someone who will be in our life for the next twelve to fifteen years.

Afterwards, I went to the town animal shelter, where it's easier to walk away because most of the dogs there are older, or sick or have behavioral issues. There's a stark contrast between the high-bred expensive puppies who know they're young and cute and have the world by the tail, and the ones in the shelter, many of whom were once those puppies, now discarded. They are sad, beaten down, a lot of them, by life.

It was like the difference between talking to high school seniors who just know they're going to set the world on fire, who have the "My Future's So Bright I Gotta Wear Shades" attitude. Compared to people who have reached middle age and are asking, "What happened to my life?" Maybe that's the problem with my trying to date now, at forty-two. In my twenties everyone had a lot more enthusiasm. Now they're just downtrodden. Not everyone, just the ones I seem to attract. Hence, the moratorium on human dates.

There was one dog I saw, an old Beagle. He's been there a long time with his best Beagle friend. It could be his brother; I'm not sure. They have to be adopted as a set. At my age, a lot of men have those same restrictions, be it with exes you have to deal with forever, or their parents, extended families…A lot of those men remain "unadopted" as well. I feel bad for them but won't take them home either.

I went home and ate a *Smart Ones Enchilada* for lunch and patted myself on the back for making it through another day without getting a dog, or a boyfriend, or eating copious amounts of chocolate. I did have one glass of Chocolate Wine (*Chocovine*) over a friend's house and it was amazing! I highly recommend it if you like that sort of thing. As she said, "It's like chocolate milk without the phlegmy stuff."

Time for bed now after a busy day.

Enjoying my new life very much so far. Feeling renewed enthusiasm.

Rebound Mechanisms and Losing Yourself

August 2, 2011

One of the biggest draws about new relationships is that you get caught up in the activity of getting to know the other person. You learn all about their habits, their likes and dislikes. For a while all your mental energy pours into cramming to find out everything you can. It's like landing the perfect job, the one better than you ever dreamed it could be. Until, well you know, the thrill wears off but you still like going to work every day, or else it's a job you hate and you have to quit. Or sadly, you get fired.

I talked to one of my friends about how she handles break ups and here's what she said:

"I had lots of stupid relationships, got heart-broken twice and even three times repeatedly by the same men. I dated all of my exes again, and all failed multiple times. Over and over. I guess that helped me not to fear much, and gave me a thick skin. X sometimes complains I am too practical and not much emotional.

After all my breakups, I pledged to learn something new. A yarn craft, a new skill. I am one of the most proficient yarn handlers I have ever met. I beat the oldest women in the family, as I do several styles of crochet, knitting, tatting, embroidery, cross-stitch and I sew by hand. I made dresses and skirts for my daughter by hand.

Men were not useless after all…they made me learn a lot."

I think she's got a good point. And one that hadn't occurred to me. Whenever I'm single I try new hobbies but never made the connection. I've done stained glass, mosaics, canning, more baking than anyone should be allowed...

When breakups happen, even the ones that end in solid friendships which most of mine thankfully have, you still lose a piece of yourself. You gain something, learning new traits about the other person and yourself, but you lose something too. A part of you is left irretrievably behind. Hobbies don't have that painful side effect.

Nor do pets, and that just reinforces my current Rebound Mechanism—to get a dog. You get the benefit and mental fulfillment of learning all about someone new, their habits, their likes and dislikes without ever losing yourself. And that unconditional love thing they offer? Priceless.

Rebounds and Impulsive Love Shopping

August 3, 2011

In my past, I've been known to do my share of impulsive shopping. I don't buy houses or fancy cars but I do have a bad habit of jumping into quick relationships with men and new pets.

Many years ago, before Ivy was in the picture, when I was still in my mid-twenties and married to Ivy's dad who was as impulsive as me, we got a bull mastiff puppy. It was innocent enough. We were driving down the street, looking for yard sales, and there emerged the sign. "Free Bull Mastiff puppies." We pulled over, neither of us knowing what that breed looked like. Of course when we saw the pile of giant brown puppies with black faces and giant paws we both said, yes, yes, yes!

Sally was adorable, no doubt, but she had major separation anxiety issues. She chewed (doorknobs, pillows), she urinated the second we walked in the door because she feared she'd get in trouble for whatever daily damage we hadn't found yet. She ate rocks, light-bulbs, and cans, and anything in her reach. She was super loving and the sweetest thing in the world, so long as we didn't leave her. Back then, they didn't have anti-anxiety meds for dogs. Long story short, after four years of our house being destroyed, and a lot of tears, we found her a family with lots of kids and a stay-at-home mom. Over the years we spoke to her new family and she was a perfect fit and very happy.

I mentioned Sally because I've had similar outcomes with impulse men who are so wonderfully sweet except for X, Y, Z issues. The issues are generally there in the beginning but I am often blindsided because of their charm. "It's okay," I'd say, "You didn't mean to eat that pillow/yell at me, you were just upset because you have a fear of thunderstorms/commitment." And I'd make excuses until I'd HAD IT. And then they would have to go. And generally, the men found new families who fit perfectly, and they are happy.

I think the big difference is that dogs only live to be about fifteen, if we're lucky. Men? Eighty plus years. People and puppies are not born afraid of rolled up newspapers or being left. They develop new fears and new baggage as they age. At this point, I'm dealing with finding someone sweet and loving and emotionally unharmed with forty plus years of learned responses to situations. And of course I've got my own emotional "quirks" which would have to be accepted and have to mesh.

In the past couple of years I've gotten much smarter about spotting these bad behaviors and running before any bonding happens. Or at the very least, leaving before he or I get even more attached. I've been accused of having "conflict resolution issues," but I like to think I've just gotten a better awareness of what won't work. My list of what I don't want and can't handle is long and growing:
- No lying
- No chewing
- No floppy ears
- Must be housebroken
- Must not be aggressive (that pertains to either species)
- Must not run away

My list of what I want is pretty short: Must be nice, honest, hard-working, and be a good stand-up guy/dog. I am in no hurry, and enjoy being alone with my daughter and Henry. Perhaps there will be a new dog, if he or she is just the right dog. But if not, I still have me.

My New Rebound Dog, Lily G.

August 5, 2011

Well we got her. Our little girl, Lily G. And she is just what we wanted.

My daughter is home from her vacation with her dad's family so today I took the day off from work and we looked at puppies. Just in case. She's remained vehement about her desire to have a Yorkshire Terrier. I remain firm that 1) Yorkies are hyper and 2) they are prohibitively expensive.

So I took her to the puppy store to look at the Puggle (Pug/Beagle and MUCH cheaper) who I thought was adorable. Meanwhile I was feeling ethically guilty of getting a dog from a front for a puppy mill. She held the Puggle, but I could see her heart wasn't in it. She gazed past that dog to the Yorkies on the other side of the store. Those particular Yorkies were hyper, male, and more than we could afford. I told her I was sorry, we were not getting a Yorkie. No way. She asked then if she could just get the wrinkled tan Puggle.

I caught myself then, luckily recognized something in my thought process. How many times had I said. "No, this guy is GREAT, you're going to love him." Wow. Here I was again, trying to sway her to like someone I liked. Those days are over!

I told her no she could not get the Puggle, because she didn't love the dog and spending twelve to fifteen years is a long time to always be wishing you had waited for someone else. Settling for the first cute one that comes along has been a problem for me in the past (men, I mean). Worrying that no one else might show up. What if that was my last chance, I'd wonder.

I refused to continue to teach Ivy my unhealthy patterns. We left the store.

I expected a meltdown but she agreed, held my hand, and said, "Good, because I really want a Yorkie."

When I got home I searched the local classified ads online and surprisingly found Yorkies for sale, for the same "low" price as that Puggle in the store. The pups were raised in the house with their parents and siblings and humans. It was a miracle. So we went to check it out.

There were two females available, nine weeks old. A hyper one and another who was shockingly calm and quiet. I had no idea that breed could produce a pup with those traits. My daughter was in love immediately and thrilled. And frankly so was I.

We spent almost an hour there, playing with the puppy, and finally agreed that this was the puppy for us. Ivy named her Lily. Lily keeps trying to cuddle with Henry. He's not very welcoming but I think he'll warm up soon. He hissed twice but hasn't scratched her with his chubby kitty claws.

So, lessons learned today? How can I translate this puppy experience to human relationships?

It is better not to settle because the one you should spend your life with might be just around the next bend.

If I ever do date again, which clearly I have no interest in presently, then I should be more open-minded. I was resistant to the idea of this breed because of my misconceptions. Perhaps there were men over the years who never crossed my radar for the same reason. Moot point though because Lily will keep me plenty fulfilled for some time.

Listen to your children. Ivy has never wavered in what she wanted. And now that she has it, she is beyond happy.

Don't force your beliefs or choices on your children. Let them want what they want, and respect it.

Don't be afraid to change your mind, to admit you're wrong, and to follow a new path.

I am enjoying my new path, enjoying using what I've learned from my mistakes to make this the best life it can be for me and for my little family, now larger by one.

Match.com v.s. Petfinder.com

August 6, 2011

In the past handful of years I've spent way too much time on both Match.com and Petfinder.com. They have a lot in common. Both of them:

• Offer you a chance to search for someone to love

• Help you narrow your choices by location, breed/race, age, size, gender

• Allow you to expand or change your search if no one good comes up

• Grant you access to hundreds of profiles so you can spend a whole Saturday night weeding out the "no ways" and trying to find even one or two "maybes."

Sadly, both also often post ads that can be misleading. A friend of mine found a Yellow Lab on Petfinder. She was quite excited with her find, fawned over his picture, and arranged to adopt him after a thorough background check and series of questions similar to those on Match.com or similar sites.

It was a long distance relationship, with the dog to come from TN. On a lark, because she'd been burned in dishonest love relationships in the past, she asked that the vet neutering him, check his DNA. Guess what? He wasn't a Lab at all, but mostly Pit Bull. It's a bum rap because I know some wonderful Pit Bulls, but the fact is, she was lied to and the relationship was over. Who knows what else the previous owner lied about?

So many people who post profiles to computer dating sites are clearly not telling the truth. I dated one guy after two months of online chat and phone calls. He lied about his height, hair, relationship history, upbringing, job...

What I don't understand on any of these human or dog dating sites, is why lie? Eventually whoever falls in love with you is going to find out who you really are. Bait and switch isn't a good foundation for a long-term relationship.

Petfinder makes it easier to filter, and for the most part I think those ads are more honest. They have symbols for their restrictions. Having those on Match.com would eliminate a lot of wasted time. They could have symbols that represented:

• Just out of marriage
• Never been married
• Doesn't like kids or pets
• Health issues
• Trouble socializing.

Dating is not a perfect system, nor is pet adoption. Be careful. Meet your prospective dog/cat/human before you commit. Find out the truth. Come to think of it, wouldn't it be great if you could get the "CarFax" for people?

Have a wonderful weekend

Breakup Recovery 101

August 9, 2011

When my first real boyfriend broke up with me, back in high school, it was devastating. I didn't know which end was up and I was sure I'd never get over it, never stop being sad. I did get over him, of course. In the words of Sheryl Crow, the first cut is the deepest. Subsequent breakups hurt, but it got easier. I realized that when a relationship ends, the world doesn't.

Fast forward twenty-seven years later. I really thought this recent person I was in a relationship with was "the one". And when it ended, rather abruptly, I was crushed. For a few days. Then I was mostly okay with occasional bouts of sad. Nothing really bad though. I didn't miss work or overeat or drink too much.

What I've learned over the years is that people come and go. Sometimes you meet a friend and he or she is in your life forever. Other times, it's a few months or a few years. We think everyone will be with us forever. But there are moves and marriages, and college and divorces, and death. And we have to start over, make new friends, create new families. It's the stuff you surround yourself with before and during the relationship that will carry you though. Children, jobs, friends, hobbies, family, and of course pets are huge diversions. They can bring great amounts of joy.

If you look for it, there are smiles all around. Most people miss them but look carefully, think sunny thoughts, and you'll be surprised where happiness is hiding.

This morning before work as I was walking Lily, I heard guitar music in the distance. I walked toward my new neighbor's place. I live in a townhouse and a month ago my old neighbors moved away. I was disappointed because I'd become quite close to that couple. My ex-boyfriend played guitar and since he is also recently out of the picture, I was lamenting the loss of live acoustic guitar music in my home. But there was my new neighbor, Kim, sitting at a table and chairs in her garage strumming and singing a quiet ballad. I walked over and smiled, told her thank you and said hearing her play was a relaxing and wonderful way to start my day.

I followed it up with kissing my new little puppy who is doing great with her housebreaking by the way. I dropped Ivy off at camp after that, thankful to have such a great daughter.

There is plenty of beauty in the world, a plethora of good things tossed in our path to remind us that we are not alone, that life is good and wonderful even when occasionally someone we've grown attached to has to leave.

And of course, there is no shortage of puppies in this world. If you can't have one, go to your local shelter or puppy store and hug one. Their wagging tails are all the proof anyone should need of hope.

Losing Weight- Ready, Get Set, Go!

August 10, 2011

I went back to the gym today after a three-week hiatus. I've never been the gym type. I loathe exercise. Some people get an adrenaline rush, love the tearing of their muscles, no pain no gain and all that. I only go when I have to, when the long winter of homemade candy making, and stuffing and mashed potato dinners have warped my body.

Of course there are other seasons to blame. Spring, coming in like a lion with Easter candy clearance sales and blasted Cadbury Creme Eggs. And then summer of course with summer-only ice cream stands and strawberry shortcake. I don't sleep much in the summer either so there's the 3pm Snickers pick me up habit I sometimes fall into at work. And back to autumn and the smell of cinnamon and falling leaves and hence the constant urge to can jams and apple butter.

And that brings me to where I am now. Happy with things, accepting of my lot in life and grateful for what I've got. But slightly not so happy with my middle. I'm okay, can pass for fine. My doctor, bless his heart, has never told me I need to lose weight. My vital stats are in line with where they should be.

But certainly a little toning up will be good for me. I'd like to lose twenty pounds but realistically, I know myself too well and that kind of weight loss will involve severe calorie restriction. I don't want to lose the weight that badly to be hungry for the next three months. I get very cranky when I'm hungry despite six small meals a day,

So for now I'll shoot for ten pounds or for last summer's clothes to fit me again, whichever comes first.

Here's hoping for success in my quest.

Let Sleeping Dogs Lie or Dig Them Up

August 13, 2011

There's nothing so cute as a sleeping puppy. Because they're adorable and content and innocent, it's tempting to pick them up and kiss them. It's like picking at a scab. Or trying to dissect what happened in an ended relationship.

I'm guilty on all counts. Well, I don't pick scabs but the other two. I smother Lily in kisses all the time when she's napping, and with exes there's always a postmortem performed. What happened? Whose fault was it? What did I learn from this experience besides "Don't date, ever again!"

I've found there are two types of people: those who stay amicable with their exes and those who don't. I've grown suspicious of those who never have any contact with the ex-wives or who only speak through lawyers. Sure, maybe their exes were troublesome, but without communication, there's no way to really tell. Not that I want an ex flitting around, and certainly my exes' new fiances and wives must hate that I'm bouncing around, being a friend. But I think it's important.

When you hire someone for a job, you can ask the old employer questions, and legally they're probably not going to tell you the truth. But they can hint: Joe really liked to work alone (not a team player). Or how about, Well we never had to worry about Joe working too many hours (he was lazy, run while you can). His strength lies in his communications skills (flirt). He's creative and thinks out of the box (bullshitter, dreamer), and finally He's happier working at his own pace (stubborn).

If a man puts in his resume, "Do not contact my old employers, they're all crazy and they lie!" or "They fired me because they don't know how to work with me," then you're not going to hire them right? They won't get past the first interview/date. So if they say that about their exes, should we believe them? Personally, I'd prefer an ex or two to tell me he's a good guy overall but not a good match. Maybe there's more to the story but if his exes are friendly to him, how bad could he be?

And YIKES, beware the rebound. If they just broke up and the ex is around, also not good.

It's a lot to think about but this next time, if there is a next time, I'll be better prepared.

Happy Friday!

Finding the Right Breed For Your Needs

August 15, 2011

Puppies need to be stimulated all the time. They like to play, to chase and be chased. They run and bark and chew things. They thrive on adrenaline. When you ignore them or when the fun stops they can become forlorn.

That got me to thinking about men who thrive on chaos. I've been with too many of those. I meet them and they are so relieved to have met me. "My ex was nuts," they say. "I had to take care of her X habit," or "All we did was fight and I hate fighting." "You are a breath of fresh air, so easy to get along with." A common thread is that they insist, "I hate drama!" I can't tell you how many dating site ads have, "Please, no drama" in their profiles.

Yet after several months of easy breezy no fighting, no arguing, again and again these chaos-resistant men become edgy and depressed, anxious. They pick fights, sabotage the relationship, or their jobs. Often they try to engage me, to fight. One man actually paced back and forth, his hands shaking. He wanted to have a yelling match with me but I refused. I instead sat calmly. He looked ready to implode and I was frightened, so left. I've been puzzled by this repetitive behavior for years.

It wasn't until I got my puppy though that it hit me. I reviewed the successful relationships of people I know. There's a lot of drama and strife in those couplings. Some spouses cheat or drink or have troubled kids. Or they suddenly adopt children just when their lives calm down and their biological children have grown. Or they get unexpected live-in grandchildren. There are job losses or in-laws or foreclosures. And they plod along, close as ever riding out the rough times and savoring the few and far between peaceful moments.

I hear from men that living with their exes was intolerable, their lives were too chaotic, but me and my "no waves," approach is a situation they also can't handle. So where's the balance? Do I need to interject strife and drama into a human relationship to make it work? I think no, that with a healthier man, one who truly does not want drama, that he might like a little boredom, might like a life that, except for unavoidable life events, is pretty damn calm. I know I would welcome it. Just as there are some dogs who are content just to be around you, who play with their own toys or pet friends when you're at work but give you center billing at night, there are other breeds who will never be happy to sit still. Those dogs will become aggressive without enough exercise. They will pace back and forth, trying to engage you when you just want to relax and watch a movie.

In summary, for me, it's a matter of choosing the right human "breed," the kind with the correct temperament for my needs and my particular temperament. For example, Labs or Golden Retrievers are great for some people, but not me. And I've been with way too many men who exhibit Beagle traits: forever restless, jumping out of their skin, anxiety, possessiveness.

I love my puppy Lily, who I'm sure will mature into a quiet little calm thing. If not, I'm happy to toss a ball for her or play tug of war. But finding the right human is going to be a lengthy scientific process this next time. No more "Look at that cute little face!" mentality or "Let me rescue you from the shelter and give you a place to live."

Perhaps there is the right man out there for me, but right now I can't be bothered. It's PUPPYTIME!

What You See Is What You Get

August 16, 2011

Husband #2 once went through a phase where he was sickeningly sweet, to show me that indeed, I would not like it. At the time I had complained he wasn't affectionate enough and didn't give me adequate attention. So he walked around the house and spoke in an exaggerated manner. *Don't you look pretty today, I missed you so much, tell me all about your day, tell me everything! I made you a nice dinner, spent all day thinking about you!* Within about ten minutes I conceded, asked him to please stop. "I get it," I said. "I don't want your whole world to revolve around me!" He backed off and smiled like the cat who swallowed the canary.

I find dogs can be hot and cold as well. Lily can be absolutely all over me, wriggling and puppy-crying in much the excited tone as X had that day. I *missed you! You're home! Yay! Loveouloveyouloveyou!* But then she plays with her toys or I give her a bone. And though she might deign to sit next to me on the couch, thoughts of me are a million miles away. And that is fine because at the base of it, we're stuck together and happy and secure.

Lily may have some human traits but she would not wake up one day and say something along the lines of, "You know, I think I might have more fun at another house. I'm bored. I don't get enough treats here."

People adopt shelter dogs all the time and those animals generally are quite happy and grateful to have found a warm home filled with love. They don't carry on about their old humans and how wonderful they were. "I can't believe she gave me up, can you? Look at me. I'm lovable and adorable. Who wouldn't love me?" I'm sure too many of you have heard that exact dialogue out of the mouths of humans still stinging from rejection. And then you have to reply with, "That person was stupid. You're great. You ARE lovable!" Of course, often later on you discover the same hidden traits as that other "bad person" did and then you send your buddy packing.

Dogs live in the here and now. They love with everything they have, in the present. And if you have to separate from them they are sad, but they adjust and they move on. They may rack up neuroses just like us but their biggest strength is honesty.

If they go to a new home they're still going to chew or bite or hide under the bed. And hopefully with training they'll relearn better behaviors a/k/a therapy for humans. (As an aside I find the recidivism rate is about 85% for humans turning back into a jackasses soon after their "retraining/answer to the therapist/seek help to appease you" period is over). Dogs have a much higher success rate with retraining.

What sets dogs apart in this "new home/relationship" scenario is that what you see is what you get.

A few months or a year in, once they're comfortable, for better or for worse, they don't turn into a whole different dog.

Wouldn't it be great it humans were the same way?

Knowing Your Limits

August 17, 2011

My cat Henry weights thirteen pounds. He's old and cranky. He likes what he likes and can't be bothered to pretend otherwise. He used to go outside but now he stands on the step when I'm in the yard and runs inside when I do. He's declawed and knows the neighbor's dog was sprayed by a skunk last year. Plus we live on a busy street so there are the noisy cars and "that motorcycle" always making scary sounds. He knows his limits and is content to live within them.

I know my limits too. I will never be: a ballet dancer, a rocket scientist, any sort of mathematician, a race-car driver, a politician, a cop or firewoman, a scuba diver...well I could go on and on but I know my limits too. I admit I'm one of those people who will push ahead in situations where others say I will fail, but that's not ignoring my limits. That's ignoring their idea of my limits. I tend toward rationality.

Lily, on the other hand, is three pounds and doesn't have any clue to her size. She hasn't learned to fear anything yet. She doesn't comprehend consequences. She thinks the "pee pad" is just for pee, and that poo should go in places like behind the recliner where no one can find it, not considering that she might earn herself a smaller wandering area. She jumps continually on a cat four times her size with no thought that she could get clobbered. Frankly, I think she amuses Henry when he's not thoroughly annoyed by her energy and fierce determination.

I dated one guy who was always saying, "You can do it, reach beyond yourself. Push to be better!" I kind of liked me the way I was so that didn't work out. I've dated others who were so afraid of their self-imposed structures that there was no flexibility whatsoever and the idea of doing anything out of the norm crumbled them into a million little pieces of neurotic cookie. In those relationships, in retrospect, I was the one saying, "Reach beyond yourself, push to be better!" Karma.

Now that I've been on both sides of it, knowing what I am and am not capable of, knowing where I'm flexible and open to change and where there is no chance, I've gained a good perspective. I watch Henry and Lily interact. There's a lot of puppy barking and old cat meooooooooowing and swatting. And I think "Wow, I've had relationships like that."

Next time, I think I'll keep my eye out for someone who knows his limits and who shares roughly the same limits as me. Practical flexibility and shared neuroses (I mean, uh, ideals). Someone who can fight for what he believes in but doesn't have to fight all the time to fill a chaos void. No one should try to change anyone else, and so finding someone who's already just right is the best plan.

And I have Henry and Lily to remind me how relationships go when you mix opposites. Hiss, bark, swat, yelp!

Been there, done that. I'm looking for a life of tail wagging and purring, thank you very much.

Finding Your Sense of Home

August 19, 2011

I'm off topic tonight as I won't be making any dog analogies, but I made a discovery about myself I wanted to share. It's about finding my sense of home after a lifetime of searching.

I got my first place when I was eighteen, a very small attic apartment. It was on the third floor, had only two windows, slanted ceilings, a bathtub but no shower. I doubt it was bigger than four hundred square feet. At that age I didn't know about square footage. I loved that place. I made it my own. I had a twin mattress on the bedroom floor. I bought some tables from yard sales. I made a painting with my cat's paw prints.

I bought a tiny tree for Christmas.

I'd stay up really late at night and write on my high-tech Magnavox Word Processor and listen to Billie Holiday. On Saturday mornings I'd watch PeeWee's Playhouse. I had two jobs and went to night school. Maybe I was a little manic but I felt like life couldn't get any better.

Then I met someone and we got married and moved from there and lived in a series of places. None of them felt like home. We had Ivy, I got divorced, and I bought a new place. It was a Saltbox in horrendous condition. The inspection report was filled with notes and warnings about asbestos and an unstable foundation but I loved it right away. Finally I had a sense of home again. I decorated it the way I wanted. Ivy was too little to help then. I stayed up late and wrote on a Gateway Laptop and listened to Billie Holiday and thought life couldn't get any better.

Then boom, I did it again. Got married, got divorced. "He" ended up keeping the house because he spent a small fortune completely renovating it. I was heartbroken because I was sure I'd never feel that sense of home again. Of course with the renovations, it wasn't the same house anymore anyway. All the charm was lost. It became a sprawling showpiece. Lost were the built-ins and the wooden beam in the ceiling that dripped sap, and the derelict chicken coop, and the well. It had been transformed into something that was no longer a part of me. Except the mailbox. There was sweet little white mailbox reminiscent of how the house used to be, the one underneath which was buried. I still get sad when I see the mailbox. It's funny how things affect you.

Fast forward four years. For the first two I was here, I hated it. Once I signed the mortgage papers I regretted it. What had I done, buying a modern townhouse? No yard, no spot for a proper mailbox. It felt like I was living in a luxury hotel. Wall to wall gorgeous but no heart. I kept meeting men who had real houses and on some level, now that I look back honestly, I thought I could siphon off their sense of home that I lacked. Tap into their fullness of life and appreciation of where they lived. Of course those relationships didn't work out.

Then last fall, almost a year ago, I realized that all this house was lacking was my presence. I had never accepted I'd stay here. I was just biding my time till I found Prince Charming to take me to my real house. Once I realized that though, I saw the charm and the potential that everyone else already knew was here. So I decorated it like crazy, lots of paint and furniture I like, and now I'm sort of sick of Billie Holiday so I did play the CD for old times' sake but it's so damn depressing! And now I write on a Mac.

Suddenly I started attracting men who used to be like me, who were looking for someone to make them a home, to supply them with the elusive sense of home that I owned. And duh, all this just occurred to me today. I was thinking I wouldn't want to leave here for anything because I really love where I live. From the town, to the property, my neighbors, the schools.

So this next time I meet someone, when Lily and Henry and Ivy and I are ready, I'm going to look for someone who loves his home and his place in life as much as I do. I think that will be a really good start.

Just Drawn
That Way

August 23, 2011

One of the best lines in Who Framed Roger Rabbit is when goofy Roger's voluptuous human wife Jessica Rabbit says, "I'm not bad. I'm just drawn that way."

We know if you teach a dog to be vicious, to rip out the throat of an attacker, he will. If you teach him to guide the blind, his core of being will revel in being a gentle caregiver and helper. He'll learn good and bad behaviors from other dogs: barking, house training... It's basic conditioning.

If a human boy sees his father abuse women, he probably will when he grows up, or on the flip side if he sees respect and love, he'll treat his wife with affection. Kids learn to be selfish or rude, or to steal, or to have a poor work ethic from their parents.

But with some traits, you have to wonder if they're learned or if those people are just wired differently.

I have a friend who is a paranoid schizophrenic. He wasn't always that way. It was pretty sudden and has gotten worse over time. When it started though, he became obsessed with the government, their oversight into too much of his life, their constant attempts to control him, to spy on him...and he started filling notebook after notebook with conspiracy poetry. Being young, I thought this was unique.

But watch any movie or program about paranoid schizophrenics, or read a book, or visit a mental hospital. Their claims and fears are almost identical. This friend met a woman during a recent stint in the hospital and he said to me, "She's got the same problem as me, you know, with the government. They keep breaking into her computer." I felt sad for him. But here's the thing, he didn't learn this from a book, what to fear. Or from his parents. It's just there. Inside. And if you took his notebooks or those of ten others, you could probably swap back and forth and find uncanny similarities. Everyone doesn't write poetry and I'm not a psychologist so I'm sure there is a lot I'm missing here, but it is something to wonder about.

I watched a dog documentary the other night that demonstrated the purposeful inbred commonalities amongst breeds. Beagles like to hunt, and Labs like to swim and fetch things. Yorkies like to sniff the ground and zip back and forth looking for rats. Border Collies like to herd things.

And in line with that, there are some men who do things seemingly by rote, without any conscious decision on their part. Were they bred to be Trouble? They don't set out to be selfish or to mood swing. Maybe they inherited it from their parents, who sought each other out because of common traits. Did they create purposeful or unintentional inbred commonalities?

After my last break up I looked over some emails from the abrupt end of the relationship. I compared them to email conversations he'd had with his ex, printed emails he'd previously shared with me. There were startling similarities. I dug out some old emails from another of my exes. Wow. You could swap many of the passages into any of the conversations and it would be tough to distinguish which guy was talking to which girl. I mentioned this anomaly to a friend of mine who spent too many years having dalliances with others from the Trouble breed. Yikes. She recognized the phrases, as some of her prior pals had used the same ones, almost verbatim. And surely they will use them again, and again, not realizing that they are not as unique as they think. Their internal scripts are prewritten, like the conspiracy poetry.

They are not bad, they are just drawn that way.

Just the same, personally, I am choosing not to play fetch or chase or go for walks with that particular breed any more. I'd rather just hang out with my Yorkie.

The 21 Day Rule

August 26, 2011

They say it takes twenty-one days to learn a new behavior or break a bad habit. I can't find evidence of it anywhere. But everyone online and who I know believes it and that's good enough for me. It's been a little over three weeks since my boyfriend and I split up all the way. We broke up a month ago but it took a week for him to concede that we were over. The emails and conversations and lack of eye contact, or any contact, didn't sink in. Anyway, it's been three weeks since we were totally done, since he stopped coming by or emailing. A little over twenty-one days.

What I've noticed in break ups is that whoever is the ender has no problem adjusting, almost immediately. Like the second HE does something to break the camel's back.

No looking back, and it's total euphoria that you dodged a bullet. In some ways it's the same feeling as a near death experience but without the white light or visiting with relatives long passed. Instead, you appreciate what you had before you met him, what you retained. You look back at the stuff you missed the first time around, the bad traits that were clear as day to your friends and family. And you count your blessings to have come out intact with your life and chance for hope waiting patiently like a mom with a plate of cookies.

But the other person has to suffer through at least that first few weeks of denial. I've been on both sides. This time, the adjusting for me only involved getting used to changing into my skull Happy Bunny PJs as soon as I got home from work, wearing my glasses more than my contacts, and eating mostly cereal and cheese and crackers for dinner.

I confess I still sleep on "my" side of the bed. Henry and Lily are on the other side.

But there was someone about a year ago who left abruptly and I spent at least three weeks pining for him. I'd wake up in the middle of the night, relieved it was dark because then I couldn't see that he wasn't there and I could pretend. Honestly, I was a love sick puppy. Every day I'd awaken and still be sad. I'm a very rational person and I'd think, "How can I STILL be sad?" It was a little after twenty-one days though that all of a sudden I felt okay. Stronger. Hopeful. As an aside, he came back around day twenty-eight and I was reluctant but gave it a chance. Of course he left again and it wasn't as hard the second time. Note to self: Don't date clowns.

Anyway I have to think there's something to the twenty-one day rule. Your mind can get used to anything, one way or another, in three weeks. So be careful what you get yourself used to. There's a lot of potential for love, alone or with friends, or in a relationship. Don't sell yourself short. I'm not going to.

I've had Lily twenty one days today and she is a habit I just adore!

How Do You Know He's "The One?"

September 4, 2011

A couple of years ago I was single and content to be unattached. I was with a group of associates waiting for a couple more people to arrive for our meeting. The pub door blew open and strong rays of sun poured through the door, enveloping someone. Through this sunshine cloak I began to make out a person. The door shut and there stood a man in a dark long wool coat, sunglasses. His long blond hair flowed around a handsome face. He took my breath away. Till then, someone who looked like he walked out of an MTV rock video wasn't my type. I preferred nerds. But there was something immediate and all-encompassing about him. Maybe it was that he was a rock guitarist with all the charm and intoxication that accompany musicians.

I was more shocked when he walked to the table and said hello. He was part of our group, someone I'd never met. There was so much chemistry between us and I instantly felt like we should be together, or already were. Long story short we dated and it was amazing. We split up. He came back. We split up. It's been well over a year since then and yet there is still the pull, the draw on my end, even though we're not together. He's back with his long-time girlfriend and that's probably where he belongs. But what is it about some people that make us throw caution to the wind, who root themselves so deeply in our hearts that even after other long-term relationships come and go, we're still frozen in their memory? We keep poems or pictures hidden in a book or a drawer and every so often glance at them and remember...

Husband # 2 often talked about an Italian girl he dated back in college. He was in Florence for the summer and Marielle stole his heart. I argued it was the unrequited aspect of her that mesmerized him. Maybe it was or perhaps she was in his "one that got away."

This quote says it all.

"For it was not into my ear you whispered, but into my heart.
It was not my lips you kissed, but my soul.
- Judy Garland.

Another good one is-

"Love is composed of a single soul inhabiting two bodies."
- Aristotle

When I was young, those were the love quotes we believed. But as I grew older, new studies were done. Now we're supposed to be separate, stand on our own, support ourselves, be with equal partners. My happiness should not come from him and vice versa. I guess I'm confused then what love is supposed to be if not connection and reliance, trust and a sense of completion. Companionship?

Shel Silverstein wrote a great book called *The Missing Piece*. It's about a circle missing a wedge and he's trying to find someone to make that fit so he's complete. In the end, instead of finding a partially formed (aka unhealthy) mate, he ends up with another circle and they roll away side by side. But so much of me still thinks there should be a click, a sense of knowing when the right person shows up. A feeling of needing them, even if it's just for companionship. There's the big quote in Jerry McGuire. "You complete me." But now that thinking is shunned. We're supposed to enter the relationship already complete.

I've had the I-can't-breathe-or-eat-or-function-I'm-so-in-love relationships (see above) and the ones that were comfortable and easy (till they weren't, re: recent breakup) and others in between. So who is "the one," the elusive man we strive to meet and marry, the one that got away? Is it the person who sweeps us off our feet, with whom we seem to share a soul? Or is that just obsession? A crush gone full throttle? Is "the one" merely the person we end up staying with, the one you don't break up with and so he wins by default? Hard to say.

I'd like to love someone so much that I do feel I need him, that he completes me, so that when it's over it's not just business as usual the next day, packing boxes and going to work like it's no bigger a deal than ordering the wrong dinner.

Until I figure it all out, I'm enjoying my much needed dating hiatus. Ivy and the pets are providing all the companionship I need, for now.

Have a great weekend.

Online Dating- WTF?

September 5, 2011

I've had these flowers hanging upside down in my basement for a couple of years. They're dead, the relationship is dead, yet I hold onto them. They remind me that love is out there and at any time might emerge. You just never know.

Last year I opened a Match.com account. I put up the standard pictures they recommend, and a profile that was honest and brief about me and what I was looking for. The first week I had 763 views and many emails that said "Want to go out?" No chatting first just wham, an offer of a date. I read their profiles, realized there's no WAY they even looked at what I wrote. And their profiles? We were NOT good matches. So I took down the pictures and then didn't get a single view. That was just as well for me as I could browse ads without being bothered. I met my recent ex there. He looked cute, had a good profile. I found him. It didn't work out for a variety of reasons and now I'm a bit leery about dating in general and online dating as a whole.

I cancelled my account, hid my profile, but it's forever there for me to access, should I ever want to renew. If I actually want to email someone I'd have to pay and make my profile public. No thanks. Today though I logged in, for the purposes of this blog. I typed in my criteria: age range, height range, non-smoker, etc.

What I find upsetting is, in their 40's (and this may not be the same for men in their 20s or 30s), many are angry and defensive and it comes across in their profiles.

Here are some examples of lines from some of their pages:

"Looking for the one who will love me for who I am and not expect me to be something I am not. I am done jumping through Hoops and expectations set so high, what you see is what you get." Can you say bitter?

One man listed he has lots of tattoos (which I don't mind) and motorcycles (scare me) and wrote "One I can't give up and one I won't so if you don't like it..." I guess it's good to be upfront but his approach is a little off-putting.

Another one, whose profile sounded pretty manic said, "Have lotsa contradictions, and can't be pigeon-holed! Outwardly calm, but inwardly a whole new world." Can you say Passive Aggressive?

I don't want someone who is already posturing himself for a fight. I think they need some quiet time to work through their angst. Perhaps they should get themselves a puppy or at the very least a cat.

Those are easy examples but some hidden things I've seen, and learned to avoid or decipher are:

• If they're wearing a hat, they're probably bald. That is fine (I've dated my share of them) but beware of men who hide it. I dated a guy four times before he took off his hat. He said his hair was gray and he was embarrassed but actually he didn't have any. And I'm thinking he wasn't really a Shaman in Training either but that's a whole other blog.

• Men who talk about how much money they have-they're compensating for something else, probably looks, social skills, or mental instability. And many of them state they have high salaries but are actually laid off and have been out of work sometime and that was their "old salary" and "earning potential."

• If they list sex in their profiles or have usernames like "ItalianLover," run. Whatever their issues, it's probably not something you want to tangle with.

• If they list "Looking for partner in crime." I don't know, that just always bugs me. As does the proclamation, "looking for a good time," "Just want to laugh." etc. I'd prefer "Looking for someone to watch documentaries with" and/or "Likes to take long walks" (and yes I can get that from my dog but I like to hold hands).

My other warning regards pictures. If every photo listed is only at arm's length, taken by him, it makes me wonder doesn't why he doesn't have a friend who can take one. Same goes with pictures that are very far away but in interesting places. If you see the Eiffel Tower with a pea sized man in front of it, look out! He's saying "Look, I travel! I have money! I'm fun! Just don't look too close." If his profile picture shows him holding a beer or glass of wine, that, to me who is ultrasensitive about such things, screams, "I've got a drinking problem." Maybe not but this is my perception.

Out of the sixty or so men's profiles I scanned this morning there was only one who at first glance was attractive, with a well-written concise profile, similar interests, and good location. His profile stated, "To anyone who may have emailed me, I'm still on the fence about actually submitting on here so I'm not able to read or reply to your emails."

As am I, I want to say. As am I.

I've had some bad experiences with online dating and the next time I date, if ever, I think it'll be someone I meet the old-fashioned way, crashing into his grocery cart, or on a blind date, a happenstance meeting in a restaurant...

Till then, enjoying my tranquility and ME time (shared with the Ivy, Henry and baby puppy Lily G.).

The Three Cardinal Rules of Ending Relationships

September 9, 2011

My recent ex insisted, till the (very) bitter end, that my reasons for breaking up with him were not valid. Part of the issue of course all along was that if he didn't comprehend why I believed something, it didn't hold water for him. He said I needed to give him "reasons." I did. A long bulleted list as a matter of fact. I was sure that once faced with my arguments he'd say "Ah, I see. Well shame on me. Okay, sorry to have flubbed up your life, I'll move on." Of course nothing is ever that easy. "You didn't give me any notice, a chance to fix what you addressed," he said several times.

He's right, I didn't. But that got me to thinking about people who lose their jobs. When you think about it, it's the same concept.

People are generally dismissed from their jobs or relationships in one of three ways.

• The Performance Plan-This is when you show a pattern of not being up to snuff. You are warned, often repeatedly. Finally when you continue in your bad habits, or do not arrive at the needed level of satisfaction to your employer/partner you have to go. This was the case with both my marriages. Years-long Performance Plans. I don't want to be cynical. Many people in both situations do step up and live very happy personal lives and succeed at their jobs and look back at their past challenges as necessary bumps in the road.

• Laid Off-Because of a company (or your spouse's personal) growth, or major changes in one or both—sometimes the position you hold is no longer required. This could be because of outsourcing. In a relationship this translates to being replaced by good friends, a hobby, a mid-life crisis, a much younger more attractive "worker." If this happens you can usually get Unemployment or Alimony, since it's really not your fault. I've been laid off several times in relationships. It's sad but there's nothing you can do about it except try to see it as an opportunity for success the next time you go "job" hunting.

• Fired. Terminated on the spot because you do something so out-of-bounds that your spouse/employer can't look at you the same way ever again. This can be rather subjective as to what constitutes a fireable offense.

In my experience, after putting people on these Personal Performance Plans (and no, I don't actually call them that in the context of a relationship) and seeing patterns, and witnessing eventual failures based on these patterns, I'm a lot more likely to move partners quickly to the FIRED stage than when I was younger. If I see an action, I don't really need to have them repeat it for five years. Just as if you had an employee you caught embezzling, you wouldn't keep him on when you'd already given past employees the same chances only to lose your shirt.

Maybe that's not fair to the Newbies, the Interns so to speak, who expect to be given chance after chance after chance. But if I'm going to have a successful "company" someday, I need to apply what I've learned, to make sure I choose the best partner I can get, one who is as vested in our success as I am.

"Gather Ye Rosebuds while ye may..." wrote Robert Herrick. I'm not getting any younger but I'm getting a heck of a lot wiser.

The Last Load

September 12, 2011

When you break up with someone, and you are the one ending the relationship, not the one standing by shaking, bewildered, and sad, there is something cathartic about doing what I call, The Last Load. The Last Load is when you gather up all HIS things and wash them. You fold them; put them in a box with his CDs or books or whatever else he may have left behind. You wash your sheets and pillowcases so when you sleep, the traces of him are gone. You go through the refrigerator and throw away the Pepsi and all the hummus that isn't roasted red pepper. Maybe you toss the healthy cereals from the cabinet, the smokehouse almonds...Until your house is free of him and his stuff and his presence.

Of course each person who enters your life leaves traces of themselves behind, good things you can't wash away. Whether it's a show you never experienced before but learned to love: *Bones, Family Guy, Life on Mars, Dexter,* or the taste for better whiskey, appreciation of local Blues clubs... And there are always the bad things that all the Tide or Spic and Span can't wash away. Maybe a learned distrust of men, or a loss of hope, loss of things: money, your *Jacob's Ladder* screenplay book, the big ole house he got in the settlement, the good office chair, respect, dignity, a shared cat...

And that's why doing a purge of what you CAN purge is so helpful. Sadly, I've got my share of pics with ex boyfriends/husbands who will forever appear in various places online despite my taking down the pics. Sometimes they show up on older versions of my website which has long since been updated. But the Internet is similar to the human brain. You can delete whatever you want and move to a new location and change your name, but the memories will always linger. But it's good to at least try. Untagging pictures on Facebook is a great start. Thankfully I deleted my MySpace some time ago so that's one less place to worry about. And this time, I never even gave HIM a mention on my website. Learning my lesson.

Yesterday was my birthday and it got me to reflecting more than usual. I've become a little too tentative in relationships (so said Husband # 2 when I just COULDN'T change my last name). Just as well as we didn't even last two years and then I would have gone from Mrs. X back to Ms. G again with all the legal docs and ramifications and paperwork and confusion that entails.

I've become like a Military wife the way I can pack up someone's essence and move it out. I have done too many Last Loads in the preceding bunch of years.

I hold out hope that someday I will meet the person I'm destined to be with if I am destined to be with someone and not alone with my books and ideals (not a bad thing by any means). Someone I can believe in and respect, who I can take at face value. Someone who stands for the things I stand for. Surely there is a man out there who is not squirrelly or perpetually cranky, who works hard (and steadily) for what he wants and needs, who can love without losing himself or expecting me to. Who doesn't pretend to be perfect at first, only to show his faults after I'm hooked. Hooked or not, I drop men like hot potatoes once I know they've misrepresented themselves.

This morning when I was doing dishes, a smiley face appeared in the sink. I know it was just the spoon's reflection in the stainless steel but I like to think it was a sign that I'm on the right track. Strong and Single with growing inner happiness beats Sad and Attached to the wrong person with depleting inner happiness any day of the week.

Here's to a good year!

Dogs in Heat

September 14, 2011

When female dogs go into heat male dogs can sense it, and they swarm. They jump up and down and whine and make fools of themselves in the hope they will be the one to "bag the babe."

It has been my experience that human males react in much the same way. Once a woman "frees up," even if she has no interest in dating, men will rush to her, certain that she wants to be paired up. I'm always reluctant to admit when I've suffered a break up, or to announce in social networks that I have become "single." As soon as I do, single men make no delay to "offer up their services."

The most disconcerting of my experiences was several years ago. I'd gotten divorced for the second time. I was very sad that it couldn't work out despite the two of us trying very hard to ignore our differences and conflicts. I had an out of town guy friend I'd known since high school. I knew back then he harbored a crush on me but had managed to avoid his subtle advances. He was now married with children and so I figured it was safe talking to him as a friend. I had just moved into my new place with Ivy. I hadn't bought furniture yet so the house echoed. It was lovely, but cold and lonely and a little too reflective of how I was feeling on the inside. He happened to be traveling through my state and stopped by for a few hours. And I'll be damned if he didn't offer me "safe, clean sex" if I wanted it. I looked at him utterly dumbstruck. Surely I had heard wrong.

"Well, you know," he continued. "I've been married a long time so you don't need to worry about catching anything." I forget whatever he said after that except that since I was "single" therefore I must need "it." I never talked to him again after sending one of the meanest and most honest emails of my life. Since then, I get leery about "coming out" as a single woman.

I've heard about those woman who wear their wedding rings long after they've been divorced so men will "leave them alone." When a man breaks up with his wife or girlfriend, you don't see his coworkers or former best friends, winking at them and saying "hey sexy, woof woof" and all that. I'm not at the point yet of putting the old ring back on, but did sport a t-shirt last summer that said "Ain't Gonna Happen." Maybe I should buy several of those, one for each day of the week.

Yesterday I pulled up my old Match.com account. I changed it around a little, updated it to weed out attracting the same type of men I used to. I didn't pay or formally subscribe so can't email or contact anyone except by "winking." This is like a Facebook Poke and in my eyes equally as annoying. I did it mainly to see what's out there, if men have gotten deeper, less superficial. I added a few toned down, not all that attractive pics. WHAM. Almost 100 views in a day and several emails (which I can't open) from men (despite that fact I wrote in the profile not to email since I can't read them). I also got about 10 winks. One was from a 56-year-old and another who was 27. Sickened, I took down my photos and fought the urge to edit my profile to read "What the hell is wrong with everyone? Eww!!!!"

But alas, in their eyes, if I am single, and showing my face, I must want "it" and them, no matter what their situation or incompatibility. It's their duty as male dogs/men. So that was my 24 hour brush with online dating. Maybe all the sites aren't so bad, but this one continues to serve as little more than a meat market from where I'm standing. I am not a "dog in heat" nor do I need "it." And that is why I am even more appreciate of my canine pal who wants nothing more than to wag her little tail and hang out with me.

Once again, my Rebound Dog wins!

Mean Dogs

September 16, 2011

Last night I met a woman whose behavior was a wakeup call to me. I was at Ivy's Meet the Teachers night. She's a sophomore this year and I was excited to meet all of her teachers. They herded us along from one class to the next, each teacher giving a short introduction.

Over the years I've made a point to attend all of Ivy's school functions, be it Bingo Night or the annual Luau when she was little, and now the less frequent events parents are invited to. I'm in an odd place amidst the other parents as we live in a small New England town where people are still mostly old fashioned. Most of Ivy's parents are married. It's their first marriages and they've got strong long-lasting bonds. I, on the other hand, have had two divorces and a couple of "dalliances," or "broken hearts," or "missteps" depending on who it was with. In a nutshell, I'm "That mother" who probably gets deserved whispers. But I hold my head high because Ivy and I have a nice, if not utterly conventional, life. I've learned from my mistakes. And really, I would love to have the relationships they have; I just chose poorly (repeatedly) and didn't have good relationship skills back when the pool of undamaged men was filled to the brim.

There is another mother though who also marches in stag to all the events, who is also likely referred to as "That Mom," but she is nothing like me. Have you ever seen one of those little dogs in the MSPCA, who looks pretty but tired and overwhelmed? And you step close and she snarls and tries to bite your hand off? Or anyone's hand? She's been hurt for sure and now trusts no one. This little dog is convinced that all humans will hurt her. She probably won't ever find a home. Well this other mom is like that. I envision her that way so I don't get frustrated by how angry she is ALL THE FREAKING TIME. Last night I wanted to approach her and say, "You know, we've all been hurt at one time or another but all men are not—"

And I caught myself, realizing that maybe I've been a little too bitter of late. And how, if it's left unchecked, I could become one of those worn out, overwhelmed pretty little dogs, locked in her own emotional cage of distrust. I can't fix that woman or those MSPCA dogs, but I can perhaps compartmentalize some of the bad men behaviors I've seen, and not paint the whole gender with an unwarranted brush stroke.

There's a phrase, "If you keep going where you're going, you'll end up where you are." I don't know who said it and can't find it on Google. I may be paraphrasing, or whoever told me the quote was. But it's about the most important line I've ever heard.

I actually quite like where I am right now and am still pretty resistant to sharing my life with anyone, except of course Ivy, Henry, and Lily. But I don't know if I'd want to stay like this forever. There is something to sharing your life and things with a partner. When you find partners who take advantage it does make one leery to try again but deep down I know they are not all curs or swindlers.

I was talking to a coworker the other night who told me his dog passed away after fourteen years. I asked if he planned to get a new dog. He paused, then said he misses her but it's been so long since he's been "free" and he's enjoying the ability to up and go wherever he wants. He, like most everyone who loses a pet, will get another over time. And perhaps I too will seek out another (man) over time.

I want Ivy to grow up believing in love and the possibility of lifetime monogamy. If I become one of those angry little dogs, trapped in my insistence that we (snarl) don't need anyone (growl) and we won't share our bones or our treats…then she'll only learn bad parts of love. And certainly the good can and should outweigh the bad. If you pick the right dog and train it well, then it is possible to get it right.

Signing off, feeling slightly more inspired, and less jaded.

Back Up Plans
September 17, 2011

In every person's life there is someone we always wonder about. How would my life be different if I had stayed with X? Or if it was unrequited, How would my life be different if X had left Y and chosen me instead? I know when I was married to Ivy's dad, every so often I'd think of a boy/man I'd dated straight out of high school. When things were exceptionally rough between Mr. G and me, I'd wonder, What if I'd stayed with Billy? I've never dated a Billy so that's as good a name as any.

After ten years of not being able to work out our differences and Mr. G and I ended the marriage, it so happened that Billy had also ended his. Here was my big chance. We talked on the phone, once, for a couple of hours. But once we caught up on our life changes and our families' changes and our jobs...there was silence. Turns out, to this older and new me, Billy was boring and we really had nothing in common. He likely felt the same as we never had another call.

Time and again the hype and the fantasy characteristics you attribute to your Back Up Plan outshine the actual person. With each new relationship success and failure we learn and grow and change. What might have seemed a great quality, e.g. someone wanted to go out four nights a week and listen to live music, probably isn't as appealing if you're forty instead of twenty. Or if someone is utterly devoted to you and only you and doesn't need any friends, you might have learned over time being smothered by someone antisocial isn't what you need after all.

And really, I think having these back up people on your mind makes it harder to focus on the actual relationship. You might see it as a glorious option and if you can just extricate yourself from this guy, then YAY, you can rush back in the arms of your special X and live happily ever after, as you should have before. That rarely happens. Sometimes, yes. I've heard many stories of people in their fifties reconnecting with men they dated in their twenties. After failed marriages, they find each other and marry. But, that is the exception not the rule.

No one gives a dog to a shelter, then two years later (after they've adopted a large Lab who ate their couch and tried to eat a neighbor) tries to get it back. The first dog didn't work out, the second one didn't either. You don't go back. You make a list of characteristics you like and don't like and the next dog will better fit that criteria. If not, then refine the list for next time. (I do not condone getting rid of dogs for minor things. If they're not biting people's faces off, it should be a lifetime commitment and I still feel badly about my old dog Sally). Human relationships work the same way. You don't go back. Anyway, you can leave adult humans more easily since they can take care of themselves (or claim to in their dating ads; if they embellished their survival skills it's not your fault).

Keep making your lists and stick to them. If the list seems too restrictive, don't be tempted to go back and adjust it. You can tweak, but don't give up what matters. Okay, maybe he doesn't have to have a job, just so long as he's intelligent... Or Just because he hates his mother doesn't mean he'll be mean to me. Yeah, it kind of does.

If your wish list is lengthy and it seems you'll never find someone, don't worry. You've got you (and maybe a daughter, a cat, and a puppy). Who's to say someone who has learned from his circumstances with an equally long list isn't out there waiting to find you?

Happy hunting!

Sharing Special Places

September 19, 2011

A bunch of years ago, Ivy's Godparents bought a little cottage on Prince Edward Island in Canada. We were invited to stay with them that first summer and I fell in love. I liked the area so much that I interviewed for a job there, just to see, and planned to come back that following April and get an actual job and sell my house and relocate. Before all that happened I met my second husband and decided to stay where I was.

With a couple of exceptions, Ivy and I have gone every year since. My Husband #2 went with us a couple of times. He wasn't as swept away with the beauty as I was but he seemed to like it. Still, it wasn't the same with him as without him as he always wanted to rush here and there and jog and ride bikes. I liked mostly to sit on the deck and stare at the water, or watch our hosts' dogs roll in the red sand of the beach and come bounding up the hill looking completely different than when they left to chase after a ball.

When Husband #2 and I split up, Ivy and I went alone a couple of summers in a row and it was truly magical, just like the first time. The sunsets and sunrises took my breath away. And we made our annual pilgrimage to North Rustico to stare at the jellyfish. It's a small fishing village similar to Sweethaven from the Robin William's *Popeye* movie. One large dock, that wobbles and frightens me, is one of our favorite stops to take pictures, despite the fishy smell. We like to walk along the water there and sink up to our ankles in warm red sand.

This last summer, when it was time to go on our annual trip, Mr. X was part of my life. I was leery about bringing him, as Husband # 2 had tarnished it for me a bit. As it turned out, Mr. X was fine, the trip was nice. Except he felt like an interloper on the normally fun ten hour drive as he decided to pick then to reveal he wasn't as passive and easygoing as I'd thought. He'd tired of the songs Ivy wanted to hear and commanded silence the rest of the drive. The rest of the trip was okay. Mr. X seemed a little bored and didn't like that we decided on where to eat breakfast without checking with him first, and he had that episode of refusing to—well anyway I digress. Once we got home he said, "That was fun but do you visit every year?" We said yes, we loved PEI. He argued that we should go every other year as he didn't want to go back for a while. Ivy and I looked at each other, had a nonverbal exchange of understanding.

Without words, with only the raise of an eyebrow I said, "Well maybe YOU can just stay home next year, Mister!"

We broke up a couple of weeks later and I was thinking yesterday that I really don't want anyone else to go there and add any negativity. It's MY special wonderful place (MY meaning mine and Ivy's).

Years ago when I was in marriage counseling with Husband #2, the therapist asked me during one of our private sessions why I was still married. I said (because sometimes I'm overly logical and compartmentalize a little too well) that I couldn't bear the thought of bringing a third man to the office holiday party. I said it would be embarrassing since I'd already brought two husbands and since I didn't plan on leaving that company anytime soon, how could I ever date anyone else? She said that was not really a valid reason to stay married. As it turned out, shortly after we divorced, we stopped having formal office parties and now have after-hours, right-from-work cocktail and appetizer gatherings. No one brings dates.

My feelings of PEI are the same. It's somewhat the embarrassment factor and also that I don't want to share PEI with anyone else. Today I pictured bringing someone new (no one in particular) on our next trip. At my age any man I date will probably have a child or two so they would have to go. And how would they all fit in my Mini Cooper? And what if they didn't want to go to PEI Preserves for breakfast and spend an hour standing outside after just admiring the landscape and hoping to spot one of the local Bald Eagles?

This current feeling of not wanting to share PEI is probably representative of my relationship resistance right now and further confirmation, to me at least, that I've still got a bit of healing to do. Or maybe I've reached the point in my life where I admit it's okay to have Special Places that Ivy and I visit together, just us. Or special shows only we watch. In the past I pushed so hard for total unity but I think this is my newest lesson learned.

I may date again someday, but I'm not sharing my PEI Ivy trips. I'll add that to my "List."

Key Ingredients
September 21, 2011

Tonight I prepared pumpkin muffins to bring to a friend's house. I put the packaged mix into the bowl, then added eggs, oil, and water. I sprayed the muffin tins with Pam. Ivy watched as I poured the batter into the trays and popped them into the oven. Everything seemed fine on the surface. While we waited I read nutritional labels to her. One in particular caught my attention. "See, this one contains only pumpkin. No preservatives." Right after that I started swearing because I realized I'd left out the Key Ingredient of the whole damn recipe! Pumpkin!

At that point I had three options:

1. I could shut the oven off, dump the whole attempt in the sink, and stop by the bakery to buy a treat for Scrabble Night.

2. I could pull everything out of the oven, scrape the batter back into the bowl, add the pumpkin and start fresh.

3. The last option would be to keep baking the muffins, bring them to Scrabble Night and hope no one commented that they weren't as good as they could be, that they were sub par to what I was capable of. Friends would be polite; they would never point it out right? Sure, there might be one person who would say, "These are gross, what were you thinking?" but no one likes friends like that.

In the end we chose option #2. I scraped the batter out, combined it in the bowl with the pumpkin and dumped it into a cake pan (because there was no time to clean 24 muffin tins). It ended up fine. Delicious. Crisis avoided.

But it got me to thinking how alike this situation was with relationships.

How many times has a girlfriend brought over her brand-new boyfriend, a guy you couldn't stand, who was way beneath her standards, who maybe didn't treat her well? And did you say anything? Probably not. It's likely you complimented his shirt, or the fact he went to U MASS or had straight teeth. And then after she broke up with him, you'd tell your true feelings. "He was gross! What were you thinking?" And sure, there might have been one friend who told her she could do better, but she'd probably hate that girl afterward. No one wants to point out to anyone that they're so obviously missing the Key Ingredients needed for a good recipe (for love).

Last year a friend of mine who has a long happy marriage recommended I make a list of four things my Mr. Right had to have. She said to choose carefully as there was no veering from those requirements. My list was simple: Integrity, Capacity to give and receive love, Emotionally and physically healthy, Financially responsible.

The first man I met after I made my list, well he wasn't financially responsible or emotionally healthy. He seemed like it. He talked a good talk, had reasons to explain away why he was missing the Key Ingredients. And I was more than happy to pretend it was fine. From the outside, he could pass and appeared to have everything I needed.

But he was a pumpkin muffin without the pumpkin. It took me awhile to figure out what was wrong but when you leave out half the recipe, you can toss in nuts and coconut, nutmeg and hell, even white chocolate chips to offset the taste, to supplement what's not there. But eventually, when the ingredients have had time to cook and cool, you realize what's in front of you.

I realized tonight the importance of sticking to the recipe, of not leaving out those Key Ingredients. Sure you could add a little less sugar, or a little more cinnamon, but without the basics, you really don't have pumpkin muffins at all.

The next time I date, if the man is missing any of his Key Ingredients so important to achieve the level of love I deserve, he will be tossed in the sink so to speak. And I'll start over.

Stick to your personal recipes for love, and it'll all work out.

Visualizing Yourself to Happiness

September 23, 2011

Back in high school, I picked up a Weight Loss hypnosis CD. Okay, you got me, it was a cassette tape. I listened to it faithfully. Though I didn't lose much weight, my habits changed and to this day, once in a while I'll hear the narrator's voice saying "cancel cancel" which was his code for "Stop what you're doing and think!"

So here I am MANY years later, still struggling with weight. I'm not obese but none of my clothes from last year fit the way they should and I need to do something drastic to get myself revved up to lose a good bit of Carly. I've been on tons of diets so know WHAT to DO and WHAT to EAT. What I need is a mental adjustment.

And that is why today I visited a Hypnotist who has quite a bit of credentials and success stories on readjusting unhealthy thinking. He said since I'm a writer that the creative visualization, which is integral to the process, will be easy for me. He also said I'm not "That bad off" in terms of deeply ingrained behaviors and I just need a tweak. That made me happy as I'm generally impatient and was hoping to be "realigned" quickly. After a few minutes of talking with him and then having my session, I already feel hopeful and a little different. One thing in our conversation though struck a chord in me.

I was explaining how open I am to suggestion (buying everything on Infomercials and on end caps) and that I'd be a good candidate. Sure enough, when he made me close my eyes and then described Chocolate Lava Cake to me, in a new way, the idea of eating it was repulsive. Cool!

Something dawned on me then. All someone needs to do is to suggest a situation a certain way, and I believe it.

I knew this but didn't realize how easy my mind accepts the new reality as truth. Too strong is my willingness to readjust what I see as reality. These new suggestions become as real to me as the lives of the characters I create, as real as happenings in my actual life.

That's helpful when I want to be hypnotized or get into a character's head, but not when I'm trying to be objective in a relationship.

I had one suitor who repeated we'd live "happily ever after." He verbally set the stage for how wonderful and lasting and permanent everything was. The fact that we kept splitting up didn't register because I was still convinced we were in a fairy tale. Looking back, there have been many times I've been stuck in *The Emperor's New Clothes* thinking. Sometimes I'd believe it without thought and other times I had to force myself to keep believing. But in most situations, the Emperor was naked and I was in relationships with partners who were not healthy choices for me.

Just as the hypnotist can probably train my mind to start seeing unhealthy foods as unhealthy, to comprehend what's really in them, to stop being deluded by the taste of chemicals and refined sugars, I'm guessing he can probably train me to see men as they really are. Yikes!

I'm going to retrain myself and work hard to start liking salads and veggies and fruits because they will nourish and not destroy me. I'll be swearing off potato chip sandwiches and Nutella straight from the jar. By the same token, I'll be taking a good hard and honest look at any men I encounter in the future, and will start seeing them as they really are, for better or for worse.

Dating Ads
That Deliver

September 29, 2011

Since Match.com turned out to be little more than a meat market in my opinion, I opted to try out eHarmony. I'd joined about a year ago and at that point had filled out the very long questionnaire. This was the same easy tweaking process as when I rejoined Match.com. I updated a few pictures and changed my preferences so they'd be very strict. It's probably obvious to everyone that I've become relationship resistant at this point so any of the "not that importants" I adjusted to "very important." This will severely limit how many matches I get but will also separate the wheat from the chaff.

I hit the "find new matches" icon and waited. The thing that's great about eHarmony is that the matches you see everyday are the same ones who see you. There's no cheating and completely changing your criteria so you can see a bunch more. Sure you can change the age range a little or slide the importance levels down, but what you see is what you get. I have to admit, despite my reluctance to start anything up with anyone, I did log into my email excitedly the first few days just in case someone perfect showed up.

No one did. Not yet. I know my standards get higher and higher all the time, but better that than low standards and broken hearts. Another good thing about eHarmony is that the men in there, the ones who pay all the money to take their time and find someone just right, aren't jumping ahead and immediately asking me out on dates without talking first. They take it slow and most don't write at all. Part of me worries that maybe MY profile comes across as combative and bitter, like some I've criticized. But my friend and her boyfriend read it for me and told me no, it's fine, except for that one bitter combative line I promptly removed once they kindly pointed it out.

But enough about the merit of this dating site that is allowing me to be "out there" without really having to interact with anyone; and instead just gives me my daily possible list and leaves off men who don't meet the criteria according to their formula. And in this precious time I can heal emotionally, which is key.

One thing I noticed on these ads that I thought was worth note. About 20-30% of men list out their passion as things like "playing sports, watching sports, exercising, working out five times a week." I archive (delete) them pretty quickly. It's great they are into sports and guy stuff, but they ought to write about something a potential date may enjoy. For example, if I were to list out, in that initial paragraph which is the first thing anyone sees besides your pictures, "canning pickles, making apple butter, sitting alone writing on the couch, making crafts with my daughter, hanging out with girlfriends and talking about boys," I'm thinking they would archive me pretty quickly.

Here is what I would like to see in the What Am I Passionate About section, "Passions include: playing blues guitar, reading fiction, writing fiction, being a good person, hanging out with a group of long-term friends, and reducing my carbon footprint." That would be one I would click on. But until then I am happy to play with my kid and my dog.

There's something to be said for dating sites that let you browse at your leisure, that don't beat you over the head and pressure you into meeting someone you're not ready to meet.

Bravo to eHarmony for delivering what I needed: daily hope and time to enjoy personal harmony until they match me with Mr. Right and then I can share it with him.

Finding A Keeper

September 30, 2011

I have a friend who has kissed a lot of frogs. Most single people my age can say the same. Two years ago she met a great guy. The good news, he's still a great guy. More times than not, as time goes by, suitors' positive characteristics fall by the wayside and the plethora of secrets they were hiding scurry out like cockroaches. Thankfully it is not the case here.

I've talked to her extensively about my relationship challenges over the years. Today she gave me some stellar advice:

Finding the right person is definitely like fishing. I grew up ocean fishing with my dad, so I have a lot of experience there, too. You sit and you wait and you wait and it seems hopelessly dead. Then, wham! You get a bite, haul it up, and—DAMN—it's a dog fish (ugly looking thing that's terrible eating). And dowwwwnnnn again goes the line...the ocean is hundreds of feet deep, so it takes forever to get the line down. Then there are countless times when your hook gets caught on seaweed or rocks and you have to haul it all back up again to untangle the seaweed. THEN there are the MANY times when a fish just runs by and cleverly steals the bait—or worse yet, gets off WITH the bait, after you've killed yourself hauling him most of the way up.

But then...there's that one glorious day...when all is right with the world...and the perfect fish bites and hangs on to the line. I get him to the surface and know that he's mine.

That about says it all to me. I'm not going to catch anything if I don't throw my line in the water. But I need to be patient. I've gotten better about spotting the dog fish. And I've let go of any bitterness when one of the naughty fish runs off with my bait. So for now I'll sit by the "lake" and wait for a bite.

Happy Friday everyone!

Who Can You Trust?

October 3, 2011

Maybe I'm old-fashioned but the sites that cater to "married but looking" or "couples looking for a third" or any of the other special companions people seek out, unsettle me. I don't lie awake at night worrying about it, and I guess they serve their purpose, but I prefer the couples-only, people-looking-for-monogamous-long-term relationship services.

I know eHarmony prides itself on providing just these types of matches. That said, this week I saw two disturbing profiles that reminded me that just because someone lists themselves a certain way, doesn't make it so. I've become more perceptive and less trusting in general but these two were so obvious, it made me really look at all the ads with a little more caution. These sites are based on the honor system after all. The eHarmony folks trust that if someone says they are divorced or single, or looking for monogamous long-term companionship, they are. I however realize I can't do the same.

Last week an ad came up that caught my eye. At first glance, the guy's pictures showed him as very attractive. And he was holding a guitar. Great smile. Good age. Respectable occupation. But then I saw his descriptions and his wants. He said "sex" three times in his short ad. Things he can't live without: sex. Things he does in his leisure time: sex. Things he's good at: sex. Things you should know about me: I like to keep things interesting.

So he's a sex addict who likes to maintain a roller coaster life fraught with drama. Suddenly the look in his eyes, the Svengali "Look at me I'm sexy" glance repulsed me. Reminded me of Austin Powers. Kind of like how now if I look at chocolate cake I see yellow fat globules and poop. My perspective has changed.

Then this morning an update came up for someone I deleted. eHamony has a sort of news feed so that if someone adds a new photo or changes something, it pops up, even if you've archived them.

The What I'm Passionate About section was updated to read: I AM MARRIED but my wife now knows I'm online dating and she wants you ladies to know that anyone looking for a scumbag then I AM ALL YOURS!!!

On a later section the following was written: I am a MARRIED hypocrite using online dating sites while judging my wife.

Nice.

Yesterday I saw a TV ad for a phone app for background checks. I think it was $14.95 a month. I can see that maybe, if you're getting serious with someone you might want to run a background check to make sure they don't have a record. But are you going to run them so often you actually need a phone app for them with a service you pay monthly? Is our society so prepared to be lied to that we need legal confirmation of everything? It seems that yes, we do.

It used to be that most people were honest and you might encounter a pathological liar once in your life. That's why Jon Lovitz's SNL character was funny, because he stood out from the crowd. I wonder if he would be as noticeable now or if he'd be placing an ad on eHarmony talking about a great job and his single status. "Yeah, I'm single and I make a hundred and fifty thousand dollars a year. That's the ticket." It's becoming harder to believe what I see in print: in food ads, dating ads, news stories.

I'm sure there are plenty of trustworthy folks out there, but by their forties maybe they just think they need to lie to make themselves marketable. Like used cars. No worries. Now we've got CarFax and for the humans we've got a phone app.

What I'd like to see is a UPC symbol on dating ads. You scan that with your phone and you can obtain the ManFax. Then when they try to sugarcoat whatever it is they're hiding you can interrupt and say, "Show me the ManFax."

Until that happens though, I just need to take what I read with a grain of salt. I need to move slowly and cautiously, checking and rechecking, making sure what I see is what I get.

Ivy and Lily are, as always, plenty of companionship to hold me over until one honest shining star bursts forth into my life and makes me believe again.

Solitary Confinement

October 5, 2011

Ivy has been leaning on me for about a year to watch a documentary called *Solitary Confinement*. Tonight I opted to finally watch it so she'd back off. I would have preferred the topiary documentary but alas, thanks to Netflix, it is now only available on DVD. So I watched the show and no, it's not in any way "inspiring." Instead it showed me what I already knew. People who are isolated with too much time on their hands, alone with their thoughts, can go mad. Wanting alone time is one thing. Getting it is entirely another.

This brought to mind Henry Bemis, from that famous "Time Enough at Last," *Twilight Zone* episode. There was a man who wanted nothing more than to be alone, to read. And I'm sure you know the clincher, that the world is destroyed, he stumbles upon the town library and is thrilled—until he breaks his glasses. Irony at its best.

Some people need more social time than others. When Ivy's not here, I'm happy to sit alone, enjoy the quiet. Soon after my divorce, sometimes I would light candles on the mantle and just stare at them, as I rested on the recliner. And at this (hopefully brief) period in my life, I'll fight to the death anyone who tries to take away my solace, my Carly time. But realistically, am I ever really alone? No. I've got Henry and Lily. And Facebook and email. And there's the TV which inevitably coerces me to turn it on. And when I refuse, when Lily and

Henry are asleep and there are no sounds of meows and barks, or little girls…there are always the thoughts in my head and the unwritten or unfinished characters vying for their day in the sun. But I bet I could go awhile without seeing real people (except Ivy who always feels connected to me no matter where she is).

When I first started watching the documentary tonight, I wondered how I'd cope. Could I? I pictured myself in the eight by ten foot cell. I'd sit at the desk, or on the bed and write, like crazy. Nonstop all day, every day, transporting myself somewhere else. I'd write whole novels in weeks. But what if they didn't give me a computer? Or notebooks? What if all I had were the walls and my imagination? What if I wasn't allowed to talk to anyone, even via note, without being sentenced to more time alone?

I've been in situations in my past where I've been trapped, figuratively, and my imagination has always been my escape. Because really, no matter what is going on around you, you can just SNAP, pretend it's not real, pretend you're somewhere else. We can see how well my talent of denial of real life surroundings has worked for me in the past but sometimes you need to let your mind take you somewhere else. It's only when you stay "There" that it's a problem.

Watching the show got me thinking about my self-imposed dating exile and how I'm happy to pace back and forth in my house. For now I'm like Henry Bemis, before he lost his glasses. There's a whole world of relationships out there but I'm happy in my house with my kid and pets, and email and Facebook.

Despite the fact I leave Lily's door open on her crate, she crawls into her special little house and sleeps for hours. I know how she feels. The recidivism rate for prisoners is insanely high and when I think about it, I generally land myself back in solitary too. "The outside" aka "dating" is rough. I like it here in solitary. It's safe and predictable and for a little while at least, a cell I don't want to leave.

He Picked Me!

October 8, 2011

How many times over the years did I proclaim that statement with utter joy? He picked ME, of all the girls he picked me! The "he" doesn't matter, in retrospect. Until the last couple of years, that was my mentality. I would get myself all dolled up, so to speak. I'd chase or stand back and hope, shine as brightly as I could in the hopes that I would be chosen by a specific person. And then I'd be thrilled and keep up my word, to the best of my ability, to be the best girlfriend I could be. A couple of years ago a suitor said to me, "I'm just a guy, you don't have to deify me." He probably didn't say deify but that's what he meant.

I realize now that I probably did deify the guys to justify to myself why I was with them, to give them worth and status that in some cases wasn't deserved. It didn't occur to me then that I could choose someone myself, and also had the right to say, "No thanks" to a man if they wanted to court me. I'd date men even if I wasn't completely sold on them, because they liked ME. I'd get so caught up in the flattery, I'd just keep running with it, transforming it in my head to a glorious relationship with someone "better than me." I'd feel so lucky to be in the company of "him." Of course once it was over I'd see them as they actually were and kick myself, as more often than not they were not worthy of me. It's funny the tricks the mind can play when you want to believe something.

On some level—okay probably all levels—it's a straggling connection to my stepdad leaving. If a man shows me a ton of attention I can say "See, I AM worthy." Looking back now that's silly as Dad didn't leave just me, it was the situation he ran from (tail between his legs, unkept promises piled in his wake like Bubonic bodies). The fact he was pretty shitty about it is something I can see now too, finally. You don't just walk out on people you raise and never look back. Making excuses for him and taking the blame has been foolish on my part. And spending a good portion of my young-and-pretty relationship years trying to prove something to someone who isn't there is about as unhealthy as you can get. Sorry, I got lost in my head there for a minute.

When I get emails now on the dating sites, sometimes I don't write back at all if the sender is totally out of the ballpark. Or else I'll write back things like, "You seem really nice but I'm afraid we're not compatible because of..." The fact I'm not open to the idea of dating makes it easier, and it is good assertiveness training for me.

It's okay to say no. It's okay to be single. And it's certainly okay to say, "No thanks" just because someone picks you as their love interest.

Enjoy your weekend, and embrace your inner strength.

When All Is Quiet

October 13, 2011

I don't mind being single and it beats the heck out of being unhappy with someone. My friends are great about keeping me busy and entertained. Ivy is always a joy and her school events and projects take up a lot of time. And of course cleaning up after Lily, and training her, and keeping her from pushing Henry past his kitty limits, take any time there is left. Oh, and there's the full time job and the writing.

But when all is quiet, when everyone is asleep and the rest of the night stretches before me, and the ticking of the clock next to my bed magnifies and echoes…then it's not so easy being single.

Now I'm not saying I want to BOOM, get married or have someone taking up all my time. But when the house it silent, sometimes I do think it might be nice to have a guy around to talk to. And no, I do not mean to snuggle with as it's still hot in New England and the idea of cuddling isn't appealing right now. Anyway, Henry and Lily sleep on the bed, on my feet.

What I really miss is talking to someone late at night. You know, when you're trying to sleep, but can't, and you and your partner start talking about a show on TV, or a couple you know, or how Tina Fey looks so much like Sarah Palin it's eerie. At that time of night, it's not like I can call someone and chat about nothing. So there is just silence, except for the rhythmic ticking of the clock.

The thing is though, I still sleep on "my" side of the bed which tells me that if I met someone new now, he'd just be a placeholder, a replacement for Mr. X. Until I start moving into the middle and accepting that I can do this alone, and that having a boyfriend is a choice and not a habit, then I'm better off to just go to sleep.

I could get a TV for my room, but then I may never feel the need for a partner, as I could probably spend years catching up on missed episodes of *How I Met Your Mother*, or *House*, or any of the series I started watching years after they began.

Sometimes I rest my head on the pillow and stare up at the stars I painted on my ceiling. That is soothing. But after a few minutes their glow-in-the-dark properties fade and I am left staring at a dark ceiling while the clock ticks on.

For now I am quite happy to be single, but for anyone who reads my blog and thinks "Oh come on, she must get lonely sometimes," I do. But I'm still not nearly ready to venture out there and share my life with anyone except my daughter, my cat, and my little dog Lily. Lily sleeps better with something to hug. Maybe someday I'll give that a shot again.

Sleep well.

A Sign from God
And Saying Goodbye

October 16, 2011

Next weekend Husband #2 is getting married. Given that, I figured it was time to sell my old engagement ring. I'd held onto it for a long time, knowing I wouldn't be able to get back what he paid. But at this point, it doesn't matter because I didn't pay for it and anything I received would be more than it's earning me in my sock drawer. Friday I walked down the street from my office to the Jewelers' Building. It was raining and I was nervous about the process. The idea of moving on, completely, with the lack of concrete connection, was both refreshing and unnerving. I got to the store and it was closed.

As I walked back to the office, I suddenly realized how badly I did want to get rid of the ring. I peered in the windows of some of the neighboring stores, considered asking them if they wanted to buy it. I was ready, finally, and the idea of going back to work and having to bring this symbol of a relationship-long-dead back home for the weekend bothered me. I waited an hour and called the store. Turns out they open at 10am and I had been a little early. This time the trip was easy. I walked back to the store, still in the rain. After some small talk, and after showing them the original appraisal they had given my ex so many years ago, we agreed on a price, they gave me a check, and I went back to my office. I felt a little off kilter the rest of the day but relieved.

The next day I was on a panel at a horror conference and I saw a man take a seat in the audience. He looked just like the priest who married my first husband and me. Surely it couldn't be him, I thought. What would a priest be doing here? We made eye contact a few times and I sensed recognition. It had been fifteen years since I'd seen him. He left before the panel was over and I figured it would remain a mystery. A while later though I saw him at the booth my group was running. I walked over to him and said, "Excuse me, are you Kevin X?" He said yes and said, "I saw you speaking on the panel and you look familiar. Where do I know you from?" I explained he'd married Ivy's dad and me. We were pretty active in the church for that short period when he had just come on as a priest. It was his first job. He remembered us.

Turns out he's a big horror fan and we know a lot of the same people. We had a wonderfully lively talk and I explained about my first ex and our divorce. Remarkably he said what I had always hoped someone of the cloth would, if I ever approached them. "Well, you clearly had no choice but to get a divorce. If you wanted to get an annulment, I'm sure you could. It's a big process but you'd be granted one I'm sure." He then went on to praise me for going through two tumultuous marriages and raising my daughter alone and also for my writing accomplishments. I told him I didn't have any interest in an annulment, given I don't know if I'll ever get married again and since we had Ivy together, I didn't want to pretend the marriage didn't happen. But just knowing that even the Catholic Church agreed I chose an acceptable path, well it made me feel better.

The fact this man should show up the day after I sold my engagement ring from Husband #2 felt like a sign from God. I'm not a religious person, and haven't really been a full-fledged Catholic in more than ten years but it did not feel like a mere coincidence. To me, it was a pat on the back from Someone that I was on the right path.

So today, I decided to also trash that bouquet of roses that are dead and drying upside down in my basement like a carcass. They were from another relationship it's time to let go of. This has been a big year of letting go and saying goodbye but that is part of the process.

Purging all the parts of my life that were cluttering up my heart has been refreshing. Now that I cleared out my emotional junk drawer,

I feel like there might be room left in heart for someone new after all.
Here's to starting my new life.

Stretching Hope

October 20, 2011

A few times a year Powerball's jackpot is irresistibly high, in the hundreds of millions, and several of us in the office chip in and buy a crazy amount of tickets. Someone copies all the tickets so we know our numbers, and then we wait, excitedly. We talk outwardly, and hope inwardly, about what we would do with all that money. Usually someone, since many of us are accountants, tells us what each share would be before and after taxes. And we go home for the night, or if we're lucky, for the weekend, and get to live off that hope.

I always feel like little Charlie in *Willy Wonka & the Chocolate Factory*, the original not the creepy remake. Though the odds were against him, he hoped so hard for that golden ticket. He just knew he was going to get it and his life would change forever. Stretching his hope, even if he didn't win the prize, gave him something to live for.

The hope of finding the right person to love works the same way. There's the initial looking phase—unless you stumble across him by chance. Leafing through dating ads, or taking blind dates with all the potential Prince Charmings your happily married friends can muster. Each time wondering if the next one will be the one who changes your life forever.

And then once you meet someone, there's the courting stage: waiting for his emails or texts with bated breath to discover more about him. Then there's the phone stage, the meeting, the months or years of discovery. The bittersweetness of missing him all the time. It's euphoric, and I have to wonder if my rushing into relationships, and hence crashing and burning, is because I didn't build in enough Hoping Time. If you date someone for years before they move in with you, or you marry them, that's all time you can spend longing for them, dreaming of forever.

You can stretch the hope so that when you do settle down with that person, you've got all those happy memories, those breathless feelings of anticipation to carry you through.

From experience, I can attest that if you rush along, full speed ahead, it's a blur. Before you even know it, you're up to your knickers in commitment, and then it's over, and you don't much care because you haven't invested all that much time. You can barely remember how you even got there. If I had a dollar for all the times someone said to me, "Well at least you didn't waste years on him," I'd have a lot of money. Except of course for ones I did waste years on.

When relationships are over, the person who ended it can always tell you when they "knew." There was the one last fight that pushed them over the edge, he bounced one check too many, lost his job, shoved your kid…And you could ask them, "But he did X for years and you stayed. Why was that time different?" They shrug and just say, "I'd had it."

"I'd had it," was the precise moment they lost hope. There's always a catalyst, be it a fight over whether Eminem is a good singer or not, or someone saying, "How can you think that's your ideal weight?" One of my last straws was when I was home alone giving out Halloween candy and realizing that even if X had been there he wouldn't enjoy doing it with me because he really didn't like children. And since I had one, it was never going to work. It might be something small that sets you off, but once it happens and it causes you to stop believing, then you've reached an "irretrievable breakdown," the term divorce lawyers type so frequently, and expensively, into their agreements.

Slow and steady wins the race. I've heard that for years but haven't listened. Maybe it's time to heed that advice.

Next time I fall in love with someone I'm going to stretch that initial hope phase as long as I can get away with. I've still got some good years left in me, no need to rush.

Here's to getting that winning ticket to the only lottery that really matters.

A New Chapter

October 23, 2011

I've read my fair share of Danielle Steele romance novels in the past. The thing that's great about them is that they always have happy endings. No matter what obstacles the hero and heroine face, in the end you know if you keep reading there will be a happy ending. Most formulaic romances are the same. It's a sure bet that if you stick with it, at the end it will be worth it and your heart will be warmed. Same goes for romance movies.

With other genres, sometimes right away, there is conflict and violence and disturbing subject matter, and you have to put the book down, because what if it stays that way, with no happy pay off? Really, why read a book where there is strife and more strife and then they all die? Yes, I know there are some classics like that but in this day and age, where so much more feel good literature is available, I stick to happy.

When you think about it, relationships are like books. If they start off riddled with volatility, there probably isn't going to be big change. Sure, there can be a paradigm shift and a character arc, but in real life? People generally don't change. If it starts rough, it's probably going to stay rough until it's over. Some people enjoy that, they like the roller coaster and the mystery and hate the formulaic romance in literature and in life.

There are some readers who will stay with the book till the end, no matter how bad it is, and then there are people like me. Hit some slow patches, or too many chapters of hopelessness, too many chapters of bad writing or inconsistencies, and I'll put the book down. I'm guilty of the same in relationships.

It's taken me this long to see the connection. If I could discover and immerse myself in a "good book," a worthy relationship, where I could trust "the author" that no matter the struggles mid-book, if I just stuck with it then there would be a happy ending, then I think I could risk it. I could put myself on the line for one of those epic novels where the characters start young (okay missed that boat) and have a long life of trials and tribulations and in the end, they're sitting on a porch together holding hands and smiling.

I think my relationship failures have been in trusting the wrong authors to co-write my life story. Surely there exists a man who I can believe in for the long haul, who I can stay with till the very last page.

This is the year I switch genres and up my expectations for happiness.

Here's to starting a new chapter in my book of life.

Accidentally Falling

November 1, 2011

In the last few weeks I've only written a handful of blogs because I met someone who has changed the way I think about relationships and has chiseled away at some—okay all—of the cynicism I'd built up over the years. That's a very good thing of course, but I've had a hard time coming up with witty inspirational blogs about the agony of dating, since...well, it became...nice.

The insights we've given each other, both of us starting off utterly resistant to relationships, and steadfastly committed to not committing, and then suddenly finding ourselves in love, well I think they will make for good reading and smiles all around.

I could pop in now and fast forward to where we've landed ourselves, but since there were so many great email conversations back and forth that led to this, it's worth writing a few blogs about those, to reveal our story in the time it deserves.

I'm not sure when we met, and let me throw out these important facts. One, he lives 3000 miles away in Southern California. Two, we've never actually met. Not in real life. Not yet. I know, this has impulsive Carly written all over it. But here's the thing, it's different.

At some point he asked to be my Facebook friend. We're not sure when but I had been adding scads of people back then to build up my networking numbers. We had some mutual friends so I accepted. Last July, right after I broke up with my latest mistake, I began deleting

Facebook friends in droves. Everyone I didn't actually know, went. This man, let's call him...Ryan, sent me a message asking if he could stay, even if we didn't know each other. Apparently he'd been reading my posts for some time, as a friend, and liked hearing about my trials and tribulations. He also quite liked my Rebound Dogs blog. I was touched so kept him.

After that, I started checking his page more often, commenting here and there. As timing would have it, he was struggling with some heartbreak then. I reached out, asked if he was all right. And hence we began our correspondence as break up buddies.

Ryan hadn't posted any pictures of himself and I knew he lived far away so it seemed safe to just tell him everything about how I felt about relationships and pain and happiness. He did the same with me. When you're courting someone, you're less likely to blurt out everything you hate about men, lest you accidentally touch upon a quality they have. But he was "safe," totally unattainable, and so we could share everything without worrying that it could turn into something that, in my eyes, could mess up my perfect little life and make me have to change anything. It was win-win.

We were sending messages with some regularity, the emails getting longer, delving into our past relationships and childhoods, and one day he wrote, "I hope this is not getting old for you. It's been a good exchange for me, hearing your story and venting mine as well. You really are a good soul." When I read it the next day—as the time zone difference had us perpetually not connecting, like in *Lake House* when they were so close but unable to connect—I got nervous.

Of course it wasn't getting old for me! And the way I felt at the possibility that this was just a random email exchange with a stranger, and not...(cringing) a possible relationship, panicked me. I don't panic easily, not when it comes to stuff like this. I replied that NO, I really enjoyed our exchanges, looked forward to them.

After that, knowing how important he'd become to me as a confidant, something changed. I have a lot of guy friends and he has, in his remote corner of the world, a lot of girl friends. But there was something else afoot here, something that snuck up on me when I wasn't paying attention.

…and I think that is plenty to start with today.

Please follow me as I tell our story, as it unfolds in real life.

Today I made a cinnamon heart in my espresso cup which demonstrates my paradigm shift.

And it is a very good thing.

Switching Gears

November 2, 2011

So up until recently, I had done just about everything I could do, in my eyes, to keep myself from becoming entangled in a relationship which somewhere along the line would inevitably turn sour. I bought my rebound dog, Lily, partially because I knew she'd chew everything in site and keep me awake and make puppy messes on the floor. And surely, you can't start a new relationship with puppy messes even if you are OCD and shampoo the rug and mop the floor too frequently for regular people.

Plus there's the issue of having bought my condo halfway down the housing downturn which ensured to me that I could never, ever move. In short, my life was set up to be single forever. I actually changed all my passwords to "likebeingsingle"—well, something in that vein— so that every time I logged in anywhere I could reaffirm my solitary and fulfilling life. For a good clip there I paraded around like the cat who swallowed the canary.

And then well, HE came along. To put the situation in pitch terms, it's *When Harry Met Sally* meets *You Got Mail*. I'm of the school of thought that almost every good romance film shot in color stars Meg Ryan. I was innocently going about my business, wallowing in all the space I had in my house and the free time I had to write, and play with Ivy and Lily. I was one happy solitary little bee. Today, I was reading over some of my old email exchanges with "my" Ryan and I laughed when I saw how staunchly single I was. I was militant about it, which in retrospect I guess anyone could see through. It was a phase.

In reading our messages, it was tough to see just when I realized that the perfect man was right there. Apart from his affinity for classic horror and old movies and his eloquence and good word choices (I know, I'm a geek) there were his innocent and subtle comments that rooted in me, changed how I felt. Not about him per se, not at first, but that maybe being alone wasn't what I wanted after all.

It was gradual how we went from talking every once in a while, to once a day, to having a continual flow of conversation throughout each day so I always feel like he's with me, holding my hand, even though we've never met.

Maybe it was the declarations I put forth, my unintentional pleas to him, my shouts out to the ether:

"Part of me worries that I won't ever be able to shake my practical side long enough to settle down with someone. I suppose faith plays a role. The supposition that you have found someone worthy and you can give them the benefit of the doubt on some things and learn to compromise. It just seems whenever I do that, there is a man taking advantage. I've worked too hard to make my life just right to see it unravel because I choose poorly. I really would like to trust someone though, to get to know them really well and still like them enough to want them around long-term. It really shouldn't be that hard to find someone who's emotionally strong and independent and honest, and also cute and creative, who likes dogs and doesn't do drugs. It's a tougher combination than you would think."

Maybe he read that and thought "I'm right here! Hello!" But he didn't say that. He fired back with equal disdain and doubt about finally finding someone worthy. On some levels, I wanted to shout, "I'm right here! I'm what you need!"

There was one day we were talking about all the great romance movies and how they imprinted upon us perhaps unrealistic dreams. He said, "They are just movies, I know…but maybe it just might really be like that. Maybe. I hope so." Maybe that was the day I stopped in my tracks and thought, "Yeah, I hope so too."

Still, I kept up with my insisting that the loneliness was not getting to me. I wrote at one point,

"I think that's what I'm feeling now. I'm getting to the point that I can see it would be better to have someone to share it with. But I mean, I'm not at the point to actually date someone, geez." That was the day that I really wanted to end the comment with "unless it's you."

And I guess I should end there for today as I'm getting all romantic and smiley and my lunch hour is over. I saw a great quote online this morning that fits beautifully.

"Love is not what the mind thinks, but what the heart feels." - Greg Evans

Here's to a day filled with happy feelings.

The Turning Point

November 6, 2011

With our unexpected freak October snowstorm, I got a little behind in telling the Carly and Ryan story.

So...where was I?

It's hard to say when the turning point happened. It just seemed there were more and more subtle hints passing back and forth in emails. Both of us inching toward something, wondering how the other would react, wondering if we were the only ones feeling "something."

At one point I was going to be at a conference all weekend—the one where I ran into the priest—and wouldn't be able to check my Facebook, since I happily downgraded my cell phone. I mentioned that if he wanted to write and wanted me to check in before nighttime, he could email me instead. The next morning came and went. It was about four in the afternoon and finally my phone buzzed. It was Ryan. When I opened the email I was upset because he'd sent it at seven a.m. and my phone didn't deliver it on time. The thing that struck me most was how disappointed I was that I could have read it earlier, and smiled like that all day. I talked to a friend of mine who was with me at the conference, all about this great guy from California, who I was just friends with. She didn't buy it for a minute. "No really, he's just a good friend. It's safe, he's far away." It was the same rationale I'd been spinning awhile but everyone could see through it.

On that particular day, he ended that delayed message with "I too look forward to your messages… it's really a bright spot in my day, and gives me a smile." My heart soared the rest of the night.

When I got home later we continued exchanging messages. At this point I was still in denial, though we were emailing a couple of times a day, pouring out details of our childhoods and hopes and dreams. I wrote,

"As a kid I dreamed one day of having a big house in a nice neighborhood and a cute husband and kids and a minivan. And for a while I had all that—what I had always wanted. I was insanely unhappy. When I left him, the big thing I struggled with wasn't missing him because I just didn't. He was like a hot stove I couldn't think about without cringing. It was the house and the dream I'd always had and how now I would never have that again.

"I went to a counselor for a short time after the divorce and one thing she said was "You need to choose another dream." And I HATED that answer because that dream was the one I always had. It gave me something to strive for, and that dream and achieving it made everything worthwhile. It took me years but finally, I got it. And my dream now isn't even anything in the future or something tangible or a projection, it's just to stay happy and healthy and keep things as good as they are now. Honestly, every year when it's time to blow out my birthday candles, that's what I wish for. Keep everything just like this."

I was really confident in my answer, the honesty behind it. What he wrote back was both unexpected and jarring.

"Carly, there is nothing wrong with that dream. It's a good dream to have. You just picked the wrong guy. It is a good thing to be able to put dreams on the back burner and be content with the time. I've been able to bide my time, maybe a bit too well. But I still have that same dream."

I remember thinking does he mean he's the right guy? I still wasn't sure but it started me on a path of hope that had been long lost. I began to wonder if I had given up that dream prematurely.

It was not much later that he sent me a picture. Till then I had no idea what he looked like except for a basic description. I had written to him,

"I'm sure you're plenty attractive. Plus you're just wonderful on the inside and so much more deep and considerate than most men so you'd have to be pretty hideous to outweigh that."

The next email he inserted a very nervous and crooked phone picture, taken in his bathroom mirror (I'll note I was happy to see cleaning supplies in the background). I opened it and instantly thought, and later typed, "You're a lot more attractive than you let on, or maybe believe. Honestly, I was sort of hoping you were grotesque so I wouldn't be bummed that you live 3000 miles away."

I waited, hoping he'd get it then, that I LIKED him. He wrote back, "It is entirely lousy we live so far apart..."

After that, suddenly, the cynicism in the earlier exchanges lifted and little by little we divulged more about our feelings. Looking over all the emails, I know now definitively the minute when I grasped that he "liked" me, when I couldn't possibly interpret what he wrote any other way.

"I am sad to hear the trials and tribulations of your marriages. It really is not supposed to be that way. One will have their ups and downs but it should never be a tempestuous trial. You've had a bad run of luck and you are a bit punch drunk. This is going to change for you..."

He was going to change it for me, prove me wrong, renew my original dream. That was when I knew...

And thus far, he has done exactly that. It has been a wonderful time for both us.

We have decided to meet, for real, in person in December, in California. I suppose given the romantic aspect of it, we should plan a rendezvous for Valentine's Day on top of the Empire State Building, but that's entirely too far away.

Wish us luck, though I don't think we'll need it.

Kindness...
Keep It Going

November 8, 2011

It's been said that money makes the world go around but I disagree. In my eyes, kindness is what keeps us going as a species. The smallest bit of it can have a ripple effect and you never know when your words, or a random smile to a stranger, will save someone's life, or at the very least turn their day around.

I dragged a very young Ivy to see the Dalai Lama a bunch of years ago. Maybe he's descended from a deity, maybe not, but the amazing thing about seeing him was that thousands of people paid, and packed into a stadium, just to see this man whose main attraction is that he's kind to the core. We all felt that if we could just see him, maybe it would rub off on us. We all sat and watched this smiley man on stage talk about peace. Ivy fell asleep pretty quickly but for me that experience, the emotional contagion aspect of it, kept me uplifted for years.

But you don't have to be a god/God/saint to spread kindness and make a difference. You don't have to donate money to charities to help impoverished children with cleft palates (one I'd pick if I had more cash) or tithe, or even devote your whole heart and soul to giving.

You just have to be nice. That one thing, I think, is enough to keep the wheels of peace going.

Last week, during our snowstorm, I ran to the grocery store to get a few things. Everyone else in town had the same idea. When I finally got my turn in line, I heard the cashier and bagger (both teenage girls) talking about gum. The store was packed, shoppers were hurried and upset. It was just a matter of time before the workers started to feel it.

I pulled out my pack of Trident Layers. It's a fun gum, sour apple. I popped a piece in my mouth and then offered one to the cashier. At first she said no, then took it. The bagger refused but did take one for later. The cashier began ringing up my things and then exclaimed, "Wow this is great! It's like a granny smith apple!" I laughed, as did the cranky bagger girl. The cashier told me about another brand that tastes just like the old Fruit Stripe gum. How she at her young age knows about Fruit Stripe gum, I didn't ask. We were having a jolly time talking about flavors until I looked up to see the line of shoppers behind me. They didn't seem amused.

I spied the woman directly behind me. I smiled at her, because I was pretty smiley just then and couldn't contain it, and she said quietly, "I really like that gum too." So I gave her a piece and she began chewing it. Then we started talking about her painted Halloween green nails and how they matched the gum. Okay, maybe it was just my perception but it seemed the rest of the people around us suddenly lightened up, just a bit. It's not always the big things… Little actions like being nice and sharing your gum with strangers can turn it all around.

When everyone paid bills by check, I had mine printed up special, rationalizing that when the accounts receivable staff logged my checks in, they'd smile, even if just for a split second when they saw my "Practice random acts of kindness" message. Now I pay everything online and it's rare I use checks but I still think it was a good idea, planting that seed.

I know many people who volunteer huge amounts of time and money to causes. I salute them and I'm relieved they're out there to help those in need. But I generally don't do much except make it a point to be nice. Yes, you can give homeless people money when you pass them on the street but what they really need is kindness and a feeling that they're still human. I've got a good friend who's homeless much of the time and the one thing he's adamant about is being nice to people he encounters throughout the day. He thrives not on handouts from people, but in making them smile, reminding them that deep down, we're all the same.

My company started a program recently where we take turns going once a month to serve lunch to the homeless veterans across the street. Today will be my first day taking part. The vets will appreciate having us come in, I'm sure, as someone needs to dole out food, but I have to wonder who really will be helped more by this mission. To them, it's lunch. It's their daily routine. For us, we are living their life for an hour a month, grasping what they go through, gleaning their hardships from their unsteady gaits, their prosthetic limbs, or their damaged minds.

I will make it a point not to just serve them food but to smile at them, talk to them as I would a coworker or friend, let them know without words that despite their lot in life, kindness is still out there. After we clean up the dishes, the vets will go back to whatever it is they do, maybe hang around the Boston Common. But personally, I will emerge from the building different from when I walked in.

If you want to change someone's life today, just be nice. It's all anyone really needs.

"Wherever there is a human being, there is an opportunity for a kindness."

-Seneca

Unchartered Waters

November 13, 2011

I started this blog initially as a guide to dating and being single. And if there's one thing I could offer advice on, it was what not to do. I was a champion at picking poorly and pretending, and trying to fix. Over the years I grew a little wiser, and though I still picked poorly, I stopped trying to fix and instead took on a cut-my-losses attitude. Okay, little triumphs I know.

Some would argue that made me a heartbreaker. Well so be it. I preferred to fancy myself instead a woman who finally grasped the concept of dating, meaning after a handful of dates I was allowed to walk away if the guy had lied about everything that mattered, or even "little things" like, well, his name.

It's semantics.

All I know is that when I started the Carly blog I had some great advice to give and share.

Now though, I find myself in unchartered waters. For one, I have met someone who is honest and nice, and decent. Not the illusion of a person like that, which describes most of my exes in devastating detail, but an actual good stand up guy.

And two, I have somehow managed to trust this man so much, grown so attached, that the idea of not being with him is a crippling thought that neither of us brings up. We don't question this tangible connection we've developed, which until December technically remains virtual. In our eyes, it's already real, and the physical meeting being the big hurdle...well that matters a little less each day. At this point, he could be half man, half antelope and I wouldn't even care.

Perhaps this is the "love" concept that has eluded me all this time. The kind that makes people actually open their hearts all the way, not just a little, not just a passable amount to convince myself and others so I could justify an altar run or two. But the real thing.

I couldn't be more thrilled, of course, and each new day I look forward to seeing what happens next, the newest installment in the Carly/Ryan story. But as far as advice?

I am free falling with no idea what to expect or do. And for once, this not knowing, this not having the entire relationship configured the way I need it to be to keep myself from being hurt, leaves me feeling exhilarated.

In years past, I have gone snorkeling a few times. I never liked it since I'm not a good swimmer and prefer the ground beneath my feet where it belongs. I also have a fear of choking to death on water which I really don't think borders on irrational as some people like to tell me, since honestly, who would want to die that way? But back when I did snorkel those few times, when Husband # 2 would glare at me with his perpetual face of disappointment (and despite my warnings, yes his face did stay that way), handing me the flippers and mask, I never trusted the snorkel.

I'd float around in over-my-head water, a place I did not want to be. I'd wear a floatie and didn't care what I looked like because I'd rather float than sink. I'd put my face down in the water and granted, yes, it was really cool to see the brightly colored fish, and especially that puffer fish that Ivy almost stepped on because it was flat and we didn't know till it went POOF! But the whole time I'd keep my right hand over the snorkel because I just didn't trust that the water wouldn't flood in. Every breath I took (I tried to take as few as possible) I was convinced water would gurgle in with the precious oxygen and seep into my lungs.

I'd be out there with my floatie and my hand on my snorkel for as little time as I could get away with. And though after these unpleasant experiences I could discuss the tropical fish, and different kinds of coral and reefs and sound all worldly and cultured, I hated it. I just don't like being in over my head, out of control like that, trusting in the snorkel or the man next to me, buoyant and floatie free.

Until now of course. Now I'm clearly swimming along blindly, without a snorkel, or my emotional floatie, in an ocean filled with amazing experiences I never knew existed. For some reason now, since Ryan came along, I trust in him that each new day will be as safe and happy as the one before. Consistency seems to be at the heart of it.

Each day when we communicate, I'm happy and he's happy. I text him, he texts back. No insecurity, it's just nice. Every heartfelt comment I make, he counters with a similar one.

Part of me wonders now, if I had kept snorkeling and trusted my swimming partner back then if I would have gotten better at it, lost my fear, learned to trust. I'm thinking no, that the first time I let go of my snorkel and almost drowned, the ex would have been off on a reef alone, out of reach.

I can't offer any advice in this arena, just share what I'm learning and hopefully that will be helpful in its own way.

I think Ryan and I are going to be just fine and for what it's worth, on a symbolic level, I'm swimming without a floatie, and both my hands are in front of me. I'm breathing easy and trusting in love.

Making It Real

November 18, 2011

A very long time ago, Plato wrote *The Allegory of the Cave*. For anyone who hasn't read it, it's heavy reading for sure, but vital. In a nutshell, it's a story about people who are tied up so they can only face forward, to view shadows in front of them. They only know and can comprehend their view of reality: one-dimensional silhouettes of people walking, carrying books, going about their business.

For them, this is as real as it gets. And the argument goes, what if the people were freed and made to look at the "real life" passers by and the sun? It would be difficult and painful and hard to accept. But eventually they would grasp it, and enjoy the richness and depth of this other mysterious world, and they sure as heck would never be able to settle again for the life they knew before.

In terms of love, I've been settling for shadows for too long, most of my life if I'm going to be honest about it. And the thing about living in an existence that is so restricted, in a place where you have no idea there is an entire unexplored vibrant world just beyond, is that when you get a glimpse of what you've been missing, it's breathtaking. Once you experience that inherent vitality you can't go back to the shadows.

Now for anyone who has been following my blog, you'll know that my relationship thus far with Ryan has been mostly virtual. It started on Facebook, then we moved to email and then texting.

The first time I heard Ryan's voice on the phone, I was enchanted. Hearing him talk, the inflection in his words, how he pronounced the letter "R" when he spoke which was a bit foreign to me… it made him a little more concrete.

With each conversation, as we were learning more about each other, counting down the days till we meet, he gradually became more substantial in my life, more viable.

I decided to mail him a letter, on paper, with a postage stamp and a wax seal. It would be a tangible item that I touched, which he would open and hold in his hands. In an odd turn of events, the letter didn't arrive. I finally told him about it and I was disappointed because I was determined to believe everything about us had a touch of magic and fate attached to it. But alas, it did arrive eventually. The stamp had fallen off but instead of ending up in the dead letter office, the postman delivered it anyway. Hah! The magic of romance was still on table.

Soon after the letter, we were texting one evening. I was out of town on business in Atlanta, eight hundred miles closer to him but still impossibly far. He sent me a message. "You are home. That's how it feels to me." It was one of those moments that caused me to turn an emotional corner.

The next morning, he sent a new text. Perhaps his suggesting we publicly proclaim ourselves "in a relationship" isn't all that big a deal to some people. But it was a step for us, a hurdle, one more advancement in our journey toward authenticity. Once we were out there, a formal "couple," the relationship took on a flesh and blood substance that until then was just out of reach. By the morning's end he was so entrenched in my heart that the geographical distance suddenly didn't even seem real.

Except of course until later that evening, when the three thousand mile gap between was harrowing. We both found ourselves dumbfounded again at how much we could miss each other when we hadn't met. Well the answer to that, is that somehow in our exchanges, the late night talks, emails, texts and real mail, "we" became real.

Ryan has emerged from the virtual shadows and become a real boyfriend, with a beating heart and an essence of absoluteness. I can't help but think of the turning point in *The Wizard of Oz* when Dorothy's life turned from black and white to color, and the wonder she must have felt. I imagine it's pretty close to what I'm feeling right now.

Here's to a future of fascination and incredulity, just ahead of us, but no longer out of reach.

Old Fashioned Love

November 25, 2011

If you watch just about any old black and white movie, you'll recognize love the way it was always written into the script. A man and woman, total strangers, make eye contact across a crowded room, and they know. Or else they grew up together, were separated and reunited. There was something wonderfully romantic back then about knowing that at any minute you could walk around a corner and collide with someone who would change your life forever.

Yes, that can still happen, and I suppose single people still think like that to some degree, but for the most part, in my past, love hasn't changed my life forever. It would be thrilling and in some cases heartbreaking, but not to the degree it was in the old movies.

When Warren Beatty and Natalie Wood split up in *Splendor in the Grass,* she had a total mental breakdown. Not a good thing; and these days, when you're courting, if someone tells you he had a breakdown when his girlfriend left him, you'd run screaming. But when a relationship ends, it should matter. If you part, there should be a vast emptiness. You know you will never love that fully again. The way we, as a society, have it set up now is that if we lose someone, that's okay, we'll just find someone else. Since it's not going to kill you or cripple you because you've set up safeguards on the emotional, legal, and financial fronts, it's no biggie. You eat a bunch of ice cream, burn some pictures, and just find someone else better. Plenty of fish in the sea, right?

In the old days, you'd buy a house, get married, and stay with both forever. You didn't keep trading up for better houses and better spouses. And the person you settled down with, you might have just met, maybe just before he shipped off to the war. Maybe you only had a handful of dates before you married to lock each other in. Back then, no one thought twice about it. When Mary Hatch and George Bailey saw each other at the dance in *It's a Wonderful Life*, the attraction was immediate and permanent. Yes, she grew up loving him but it was that moment...And when they bought the drafty Old Granville House, there was no question they would love each other forever.

There's a section from the T.S. Eliot's poem, *The Love Song of J. Alfred Prufrock* that says a lot about how romance has changed for us all.

> *Do I dare*
> *Disturb the universe?*
> *In a minute there is time*
> *For decisions and revisions which a minute will reverse.*
> *For I have known them all already, known them all:*
> *Have known the evenings, mornings, afternoons,*
> *I have measured out my life with coffee spoons;*

There's something sad about measuring out your life in coffee spoons and continually disturbing the universe. Maybe he didn't imply his words the way I'm using them but if you read the whole poem, which I recommend because it's my favorite, it's about paths not taken, or taken and then regretted.

What's wrong with finding someone and immediately upon meeting them, just knowing that he's the one? Or in my case, not actually even meeting him but forging such a strong connection so quickly that there is no doubt it was meant to be? It worked for the characters in *Shop Around the Corner* and its remake *You Got Mail*. Had Ryan and I happened upon each other as penpals back in the 1950s, sending love letters and jars of jam via the U.S. Postal service, people would have viewed it as utterly romantic.

There's something tragic about society's overblown skepticism. Now a relationship can't just be about attraction, but compatibility, financial standing, and common ground. You both have to have a good education and high credit score, and not too much baggage…And there's a specific protocol about how many dates you can have before you meet certain socially accepted benchmarks.

Until recently I was on that bandwagon, with my handy dandy wish list that all men would be measured against. And don't get me wrong, Ryan meets all my criteria and I guess that's a part of it, but there is the romance and magic factor that I can't shake which makes me wonder how we all got so off track from how things use to run, when it was all about love.

My daughter Ivy, who is fifteen years old, watched *The Great Gatsby* with me a couple of years ago. That is one of my favorite books of all time. Gatsby and Daisy didn't end up together but his love for her, how he devoted his whole life to winning her over, it was amazing. Anyway, Ivy watched the movie, and it was the part where Gatsby is showing Daisy the scrapbook, explaining how he'd watched her all those years. Ivy said, "Eww, stalker!" I said, "No, he really loved her." And she fired back something typical in our time about his being unstable and that he was a stalker. And why didn't he just move on? It was a sad commentary about how this generation is being raised, where love boils down to practicality and self-preservation.

It's good to protect yourself, but you've got to take risks or else you'll never have the kind of love they did back when movies were in black and white, and someone smiling at you across a crowded room could win your heart forever.

The Home Stretch

December 6, 2011

In six days I'm going to meet Ryan for the first time. And though up until now I've been nothing but excited and happy about my trip, and mostly laissez-faire about the actual first meeting, now that it's just days away, I'm getting nervous.

I can't help but think back to when I was twelve and I met my biological father for the first time. Well, the first time I met him when I was old enough to grasp who he was. The last time I'd seen him I was three years old and the memory was just of holding the big hand of a shadowy figure when we were in a store. My parents split up shortly after he returned from Vietnam and except for one grainy picture of him in a bar in the jungle over there, I didn't even know what he looked like. When I was twelve, he wrote and said he wanted to see me (probably the whole time) so my mom put me on a plane alone. On the flight I kept looking at his picture and wondering what it would be like when I met him, how different my life would have been if I had stayed with him instead, or we had all stayed together.

I'm going through the same thing now as I look at the one picture I have of Ryan. I guess I could have gotten more pictures from him by now but just having that one, well, it's a concrete item that encompasses all of him into one tiny low resolution phone picture. I look at that one photo and wonder how different my life would have been if I had met him before. I wonder how my life will be now that he's here, how much it will change, how much I've needed it to change for so long.

And as it was when I was on the flight to meet my father, I am not so much questioning whether he'll like me, but will he love me? On paper maybe, the idea of me, but when I'm actually there? What will be his first impression?

The last couple of weeks I've been allowing myself the rare luxury of completely trusting that this will all pan out just fine, and our relationship will be the stuff of every classic love story ever filmed, every sappy novel every written. I'm not factoring in the usual doubt, or trepidation. Surprisingly I'm not dwelling on a back up plan, preparing myself for an inevitable ending. Instead I'm running with it, dreamy and downright giddy.

Except the last few days...where now I'm nervous that some unknown factor will foil this, as unknown forces have done every other time I've tried to give my heart to someone.

I was thinking today of the movie *Goodbye Girl*. I saw that when it came out in 1977. The main character and her young daughter had been left more times than they could shake a stick at and were burnt out and distrustful, much like I was when I started this Rebound Dogs blog several months ago. But then Richard Dreyfus's character showed up and both mother and daughter loved him, after much resistance. They were also both nervous he'd leave, because that's what always happened.

Over the years I've asked myself how many damn times I was going to set myself up only to get hurt again. The answer was always the same. Until I find "him." Until I find "home." And now that I have, I need to trust in it.

Everyone doesn't leave. Men aren't all jerks. And maybe, just maybe, Ryan will love me (and Ivy when it comes to that way down the road) and finally I will have found what I've missed all along.

It's been a long hard road getting here but I think, finally, I have found my home.

The Meeting

December 19, 2011

Last Wednesday night I found myself wrapped in a warm fleece jacket from Ryan's closet. I was snuggled on his couch, swaddled in a blanket, watching *Shop Around the Corner*. I'd never seen that film, even though I'd seen *You Got Mail* so many times I pretty much have it memorized. We held hands and laughed at Jimmy Stewart's quick wit and I thought, *This is what I've always wanted*.

But I guess I need to backtrack a bit, since the last time I wrote a blog I was eagerly anticipating the big trip to California to meet Ryan for the first time.

Sunday night I flew to Los Angeles for a work trip. Of course though, the highlight of my journey wasn't going to be bank meetings, but the chance to finally meet Ryan. After months of talking several times a day, it was down to the wire. And with every hour that crept closer to five o'clock on Monday night, my apprehension and nerves grew.

Ryan lives about forty miles from my office in CA, as luck would have it, and he was to pick me up at work. As I sat patiently in my cube waiting for him to call to tell me he was downstairs in our designated meeting spot, I grew more nervous by the second. My coworkers and I stood trying to make small talk, but I couldn't focus on anything. Finally my phone buzzed notifying me I had a text. "Come downstairs." And that's when the enormousness of all of it hit me.

I darted into the elevator and then to the street. Ryan was beside the building near the parking garage, circling in his truck. I saw his truck before he saw me, and then there he was. I opened the passenger door and jumped in, said hi and gave him a quick peck on the lips. It all happened so fast, because he didn't have an option to park there. He started driving with no exact plan in mind except to get food somewhere, in a town neither of us was all that familiar with. Initially I thought it would be romantic to walk along the Santa Monica Pier. But it was raining. I know, raining in Southern California? Yes, that one night it was.

So we drove down the road, headed for the hotel to drop off my computer before dinner, and though he couldn't see me in the dark cab of his truck, my hands were shaking. I'm generally pretty calm and collected but this meeting had really thrown me for a loop. He spoke to me calmly, as he had on the phone for so long, and it helped. But not enough. We'd proven our compatibility over the months, but what about chemistry? Before I left Massachusetts too many people had told me not to get my hopes up, that if we didn't have chemistry in real life, then...well, it would have to be over. It HAD to be okay. But what if it wasn't? This was all weighing on me as we parked the truck and headed up to the room. I was dizzy and shaking and really, quite an emotional mess.

But then we walked into my hotel room and he kissed me. And then I was fine...We were going to be just fine.

The next couple of days were mostly wonderful, with the exception of my anxiety about the vastness and seriousness of the situation, and my lack of sleep, and my still adjusting to the three-hour time difference. Knowing that the relationship was everything I'd hoped it would be was scary. It meant this was all real with all the implications that carried with it.

By Wednesday though, our first full day together, I relaxed and had settled in nicely with this concept of *CarlyandRyan* being real. He drove me down the Pacific Coast Highway and through a canyon road and to his town. At his house, I was fascinated with his vast book collection. I have a lot of books but he has quite a bit more, signed limited editions, first editions I've only dreamt about...(yes, I'm a book geek). He's got a big collection of DVDs as well. I spent a good amount of time sitting on his floor, carefully pulling books off the shelf and leafing through them. I was like a kid in a candy store.

I played with his turtle too and was happy that his tank, and Ryan's house, was so clean. Having been with some painfully messy men in my past, you can't imagine what a relief it was to walk into his living room and find everything relatively neat and orderly.

Before we knew it, Thursday arrived and it was time for me to go back to LAX and then Logan Airport and return to my own life, not the one we got to share for a few days.

And so now here we are, bracing for what will have to be a long-distance relationship for some time to come. It will be tough balancing loving the life I have here already with Ivy and the pets and my friends, with the his/our life that is so far away, mostly physically out of reach even if we're both only a text or phone call away. We'll have to work out the details eventually, but now that we've met, the panic and desperation have lessened. It's a real relationship, I feel secure, and though I miss him all the time, I know this is something we can make work. There will be hurdles along the way and difficulties, but we have a strong foundation.

Ryan has a replica of the Maltese Falcon next to his television so I think it's only fitting to close with a quote from that movie.

Detective Tom Polhaus: (picking up the bird) "Heavy. What is it?"

Sam Spade: "The,uh, stuff that dreams are made of."

Well, the stuff dreams are made of about sums it up nicely for me. Good night all.

On Giving In
January 6, 2012

I finished reading a book tonight where the main character got her heart broken, and then met someone nice, who reminded me a lot of Ryan, and in the end, he left. He didn't leave without cause; she continually pushed him away by holding back. She stayed closed the whole time, pretending to let him into her heart bit by bit, but it was clear to me she was faking it. I'd know. How many times had I done the same thing?

As I was reading, I saw myself—the pre-Ryan me—and cringed. I was rooting for the character, hoping that this time, she'd let someone in. Because that guy was genuine and really loved her, wanted to take care of her when she got sick, wanted to provide her with anything she needed. But she fought falling in love with him tooth and nail, refused help on all fronts, pushed for her independence. And not surprisingly, she got it.

I've found over the years that if you stay closed in a tight safe little ball and don't let anyone in you don't get hurt. But then you spend your life closed in a tight safe little ball and no one is in there with you. It's lonely. Even if you have a great kid and a bunch of friends and pets and a fulfilling job and all that, it's still lonely.

This line of thinking reminded me of that old song, "We'll Sing in the Sunshine" by Gale Garnett. If you don't know it, the chorus is

"We'll sing in the sunshine, we'll laugh every day, we'll sing in the sunshine, then I'll be on my way." It's a horribly cynical song but in some ways I lived that way for a long time. Not on purpose, and until now I wasn't aware I was doing it.

But if I look back honestly, there was always a part of me, when I was in a relationship, that looked for the red flags. Not just looked, but relied on them to show up so I could justify extricating myself from my current entanglement. Inevitably I'd find something big. I'm not saying the blame was all mine. I chose men with lots of problems and I was never all that surprised or upset when it was time to "be on my way." Mostly I was relieved to be free. To have my independence back.

Until now of course. Ryan has changed something in me, in the way I view love and relationships. When I think about how my life would be if I was single again (which is my routine when I get close to someone) I get a sick miserable feeling and have to remind myself that this time, it's all different. This time, no one is leaving. The idea of not having him around is crippling. I want to let him shelter me, take care of me if I need it. I think the period where I had to prove to myself and everyone that I was self-sufficient and independent and didn't need anyone…well that's getting a little old. That person, well, it's time for her to be on her way.

More than anything I've learned in the past several months, is that sometimes you can fall in love with someone and allow yourself to be vulnerable, and need them, rely on them and you won't get your heart ripped out, your money swiped, or be made a fool of or be left. This is all still sinking in but I'm awfully happy about it.

Sometimes, when you reach for someone's hand, it's there.

2011 was a revelatory year on a lot of levels but more than anything in 2012, I am resolving to trust in love.

Happy New Year!

Someone To Watch Over Me

January 28, 2012

I was talking to Ryan on the phone this morning (his morning, my afternoon) and he agreed that ours doesn't feel like a long distance relationship. "It's like you're just away for the weekend, but a really long weekend." Because we've become so close, it's hard to grasp that we're not physically together (very often) . I think we both forget. Maybe I choose to forget because it's easier pretending he's just at the store for a few minutes instead of facing the fact I won't see him for another two months.

We've developed this unexpected tangible closeness despite the fact we live 3000 miles apart. We talk for several hours each day, plus exchange texts and emails, but it's still tough to get my arms around it sometimes, how I can be this dependent and close to someone I've only met once.

What I've come up with is that he is Someone to Watch Over Me. It's a song, and an 80s movie but it's also a concept, a dream that up until now has been unfulfilled.

When I was little, the one constant male presence I had in my life was my grandfather, who I called Bumpy because, so the story goes, I couldn't pronounce Grampy when I was a child. He was always there, telling me horror stories, bringing me candy bars, and as I got older, shielding and rescuing me from some unpleasant situations. I was thinking tonight that if he hadn't died, if he'd been around, I would never have married my second husband. He would have talked me out of it. Same with some of the other regrettable choices I've made over the years. Bumpy would have stopped me, would have reminded me that I deserved better, that I needed to wait until I met someone who would watch over me.

He died ten years ago and in a lot of ways, I've been flailing around, steadfastly insisting, in no uncertain terms, that I did not need anyone to help me.

And then of course I met Ryan and all that changed. No need to recap the last bunch of blogs that outline our story.

But tonight I was bit emotional. Ivy pulled out her baby book earlier today and we read through it, a rare mother-daughter bonding time these days, as she's a teenager now. Seeing the old pictures and knowing that her sixteenth birthday is just around the corner was tough. After that, we took it in the other direction as she wanted to look up colleges online. Far away colleges. It's a natural progression of things, and I'm proud of her for seeking out schools that might be a good fit regardless of their locations, but it was difficult.

Ivy left to babysit and I sat here alone, emotional from recounting her childhood, and then envisioning her living an adult life on a college campus in a mere few years. She nears adulthood a little more each day. So I called Ryan and he was, once again, exactly what I needed. He told me that everything I was feeling was just part of the process and it was okay. He listened to me, gave me good advice, reminded me that he loved me. He was there to watch over me. I hung up relieved and comforted but still rattled by the reality of the future…Ivy growing up. It's a wonderful thing but harder than I imagined it would be.

Since Ryan is 3000 miles away and not here to hug me, and since spending the entire afternoon and evening on the phone wasn't the best idea for either of us, I decided to go out. I couldn't face a night of sitting alone with the pets. Struggling for something to snap me out of this mood, I went to Building 19 1/16. For anyone who doesn't live in New England, The Building 19 chain is like Big Lots but even more run down. You never know what you'll find there. I chose this store tonight because I have fond memories of going there with my grandparents when I was very little.

When I walked in, after I smiled at the wooden cut out greeting me, I spotted their big display item. Suitcases. I really need a new suitcase as the one I always travel with is Ivy's and it's too big. They had quite a selection, all reasonably priced. Since I plan to do quite a bit of traveling in the upcoming year, I snagged an adorable one.

I spent a long time in the store, thinking back to when I was a child, going up and down every aisle, wondering what treasures might be nestled in the next row and the next, all while carrying my paper cup of free coffee.

I reflected that I don't feel like I'm doing it (the struggles of everyday life) all alone anymore. Ryan is right by my side even though he's rarely physically by my side. But it doesn't matter because he's always there. I thought about my grandfather who is also "there" quite often. He would approve of Ryan. They both like Louis L'Amour, they both love me and want the best for me. They have the same first name and their birthdays are only a day apart. My heart warmed as I thought of their similarities and how much Bumpy would have liked Ryan.

As I walked out of the store, song lyrics blared on the speakers in the exit. "I'm living here in Allentown." It was the Billy Joel song, "Allentown." Many years ago, I bought that cassette tape for my grandfather, *The Nylon Curtain*. Bumpy played it over and over again. Whenever I hear Allentown I think of him. And tonight as I was leaving the store, new suitcase in hand, I couldn't help but think that Bumpy sending me the message "I'm living here in Allentown" (a euphemism for Heaven?) was a sign, a nod of approval at my new someone to watch over me.

To all the single women out there, don't be afraid to wait for your own someone to watch over you. He's out there.

Contrasts

March 11, 2012

Last week I went to California to visit Ryan again.

Though this is only the second time we've really met, this visit was vastly different than the first. When I met him in December, it was about the scariest experience I've ever had. It mostly had to do with the fact my sights were set so high, and I wanted it to be as perfect as we'd worked it up to be. I was afraid the chemistry would be lacking, or I'd drive him nuts or in real life I'd find out something I couldn't know from phone calls. Maybe his house would be a mess, or he would be, or he'd have a weird eye twitch, or he'd have road rage...

Of course the first visit went just fine. And since then we've both relaxed a lot. It's nice. Consistently nice. He's a decent, funny guy who I love an awful lot. We still talk for hours everyday. All the major discoveries are out of the way. And we're both still here. So needless to say, this trip out was a major contrast to the last one. We laughed a lot more and he showed me all around his area.

More contrasts. For one, where he lives. Maybe the vibrant colors and the euphoria were a symptom of the fact I was somewhere other than home, and I had a few days off from work. But facts are facts. Southern CA has a lot of color and this time of year Massachusetts is gray. Usually we have lots of sparkly snow which makes up for the lack of greenery but this year...just a lot of dark and gray nothingness.

Until Ryan, I had a certain ideas about how things were. Landscapewise we had green grass from about April to October or November then months of dead leaves and snow. And when Spring came and the first tulip popped through the snow, or we saw the first Robin of Spring we'd rejoice. But he showed me that in some places, it's sunny and pretty all the time. It was a contrast and I have to say I like his world better.

Until Ryan, I thought that relationships moved really quickly and were always all or nothing, right away. And the men eventually would reveal their true selves. And they'd show me traits I couldn't deal with. Or else, all the lies they'd worked so hard to hide would tumble out like a bag of marbles once I grew attached. And they'd say, "I thought you loved me for me." But Ryan showed me that sometimes a guy can show you who he is, no lies, no pretending. He doesn't suddenly go crazy or leave. And he will love you all the time. It was another contrast and I have to say I like his world better.

When I look back at my life the last bunch of years, my expectations in relationships, I can see I got exactly what I thought I would. I read a quote somewhere last year, I forget who said it. "If you don't expect much, that's exactly what you'll get." Because of Ryan, I've learned to expect more. Okay that's not true. Honestly it's been just one pleasant surprise after another. But it's something I can get used to.

The contrast to my outlook when I started writing this blog last July is about as different as the landscape between the east and west. And I have to say I like this Carly and her new life a lot better.

Orange Blossoms And Casablanca

March 27, 2012

Maybe my readers are getting bored with all the gushy stuff I've been posting the last bunch of months but I still think it beats the heck out of the cynicism I had last summer. I had an unexpected work trip last week in Southern California. Santa Monica to be exact. Despite my fear of driving in strange places, driving in rush hour and the biggest one: driving in cities, I decided to commute every day from the office to Ryan's house. It was only thirty-five miles so how bad could it be?

For anyone who lives out there, the answer is, the traffic can be pretty bad. But since I've totally switched gears since summer, taking chances left and right and facing a lot of emotions and situations I've avoided in the past, it seemed like a good idea. The first day, I arrived at LAX at noon, worked all day, picked up my rental at five o'clock and drove "home" to Ryan's house.

Once I left the crowded (route) 5 (They call all the highways by their numbers out there "Get on the 405, take the 118 etc.), I took The 118 through the San Fernando Valley. It's hard to describe the beauty if you've never been out there but it was amazing. Maybe it was my happy anticipation that I was on the way to Ryan's house, or the fact I caught myself mesmerized but the way the sun hit the mountains in the valley. Maybe it was the fact that as I was driving I laughed, thinking that a year before I would never ever have anticipated driving a California highway in a rental and feeling pretty comfortable doing so. I eventually got to Ryan's house. He knew I was on the way so was waiting on his deck for me, smiling. It was really fun to go "home" to him after a work day. It was great practice for someday.

Shortly after I arrived, we left to go see *Casablanca*. Yes, the original movie. Turns out it was the 70th anniversary so it was playing at theaters across the country one night only. We went to a lovely huge theater. I was surprised when we arrived that middle-aged people asked if we had any extra tickets. It was sold out and we had people in their fifties and sixties vying to get in. It's certainly a different world out there. The movie was wonderful, of course, as was the date.

The next day I was still pretty entranced by the scenery so the ninety minute commute didn't bother me. Of course on the way home the two hours was a little trying, as was the equally long commute the next day. My last day with the rental I drove from Santa Monica to Burbank. I had looked at a map, thought "Wow, only nineteen miles" and decided it was the best route. Not a good idea. Ryan was good enough to stay on the phone with me through much of it, guiding me through a path of surface streets until the traffic eased up. The thing that was good about the whole experience though is that one, I trusted Ryan to get me to where I needed to go as he fed me street after street and two, the immersion therapy helped me to get over my driving phobias.

The rest of the weekend stayed just about as perfect as all my visits with him have been. I got to pick an orange from one of a series of trees at a plaza that houses a library, among other things. I partially climbed a tree barefoot but caught myself and decided to just jump high for a low hanging fruit. Very fun though. The trees had orange blossoms and until that day I had no idea they would smell so good—like lilacs but not cloying. Ryan took me to some great restaurants but the highlights of the weekend, for me at least, were the visits to a couple of bookstores in Burbank. Both of them are owned by or have employees I know. Walking into the stores and seeing familiar places made me feel like home even more than I usually do.

I had an armful of books and a happy heart when I left the second store. I think this California Carly is going to make out just fine when the time comes. The downside of this great relationship is that I grow more attached to Ryan with each visit and it's harder to leave him and board the plane to Boston. Also, I'm going to end up with smile wrinkles because being with him makes me really happy.

How's It Going To Be?

April 17, 2012

There's a song by Third Eye Blind called, "How's it Going to Be?" about post-relationship realizations, when people change, when you don't know them anymore.

When I look back at all the failed relationships I've had since I started dating at around age sixteen, I think that one question has always lingered in my head, threatened to cripple me. How would it be when whoever I loved went away? I had a hard time letting go. Until last fall, I made a point of staying friends with exes, or at the very least staying civil with them, maybe sending a Christmas card or passing greetings along through mutual friends.

I did that because what would happen when they didn't know me anymore? When any closeness we had was snuffed out once and for all. For me, the thing that always got to me after breakups was when I'd run into an ex somewhere and he'd be wearing a new shirt. Not a big deal but when you're with someone, you know their wardrobe. All of sudden they're wearing something you've never seen. It's a tangible step they've moved on (as if getting remarried wasn't a clue).

I would steadfastly argue that if I didn't stay friends with the ex, it would be wasted love. I'm sure if you look back at blogs from last summer, I stated how friendly I was with Husband #2. But now...

At my age, I know a lot of people who are divorced. The current statistic from www.divorcerate.org says fifty percent of first marriages, sixty-seven percent of second, and seventy-four percent of third marriages end in divorce. That's a lot of leaving. Out of those I know, there's a pretty good and vastly contrasted mix of those who walk away silently and never want to see or talk to their ex again, those who have developed a friendship, and those will go to their graves (probably early) because they are so filled with bitterness. The third category—I've never fully comprehended how that's helpful to anyone.

There's another part in Third Eye Blind's song about finding out there was nothing between you. That's something a lot of folks can't handle. And I guess my staying in close proximity to my exes could be blamed on the same fear.

That phobia of being forgotten, of realizing "there was nothing" likely kept me from being able to fully give myself to someone new for a long time (a/k/a pre Ryan). Or maybe that unwillingness to let go of something I'd already let go of, was due to the fact that the "new person" wasn't enough. I look at some of my exes, ones who still try to contact me despite my pleas to move on. Most of them seem to be in loving happy relationships; so why do they still want to talk to me? Typing that out and reading it stings as that's exactly what others have probably said about me.

For the first time in my life though, I suddenly just don't care about the exes or what they're up to, or what shirts they're wearing. I don't want to see pictures of their weddings or be alerted if they have babies. I just want to have my happy life with Ryan and Ivy and forget there was ever anything between "us."

This time around, this person, Ryan, is enough. And what happened before, it just doesn't matter. Saying that and meaning it are two totally different things but this time…I mean it.

"How's it going to be when you're not around?" Third Eye Blind asks. Honestly, no offense to the men in my past who have put me through the wringer and I kept on "as friends" for reasons that now seem silly, but how's it gonna be?

Well so far, it's been pretty damn fulfilling and wonderful. I bid a final goodbye to the exes. Here's to finding my way home.

Ivy's Growing Up

April 20, 2012

Ivy turned sixteen recently. I didn't anticipate that changing much in our lives, as she will always be my little girl. But it seems that benchmark has been a real turning point into adulthood for her. A few months before her birthday she had her braces removed. Overnight, she looked grown up. Then she got her driving permit.

But those things didn't affect "us."

Then she got a boyfriend. In and of itself, that didn't make much of a difference, but it drove home to me the realization that someday, someone else is going to be her family. In two years when she graduates, and I hopefully move to California, she will have every reason to want to stay in Massachusetts, or at least on this side of the country. As she said "My whole life has always been here. Why would I want to move out there?"

For the first time in her life, I'm finally seeing her as her own person, not as an extension of me. That's a wonderful thing, and healthy, and as Ryan likes say continually, "It's the natural progression of things." But it's a tough pill to swallow.

Today she had some friends over to hang out. They are newer friends, not the ones she's known since kindergarten who have seen our house and her room a hundred times.

She cleaned her room all day in preparation. It wasn't that dirty to start with so I wondered why it took so long. And then I discovered something in the hall closet. Her stuffed animals.

Over the years, most have been donated. The special ones are in plastic bins in the basement. But the very special ones have always stayed in her bedroom. When I saw them, it was a blow.

"Why are these in here?" I yelled, knowing the answer.

"I don't need them anymore."

Ouch.

"At all? Do you want me to donate them?" Please say no.

"I guess."

I pulled out the two that, I'm sorry, I cannot part with. Rolo, the Cabbage Patch doll I got when I was pregnant with Ivy, and Martina, who we got when Ivy was six and going through her Civil Rights phase. She named the doll after Martin Luther King Jr. and for a while the doll sported an, "I have a dream" pin. Those two will be safe in my closet, not the basement and certainly not donated. I've seen all three *Toy Story* movies, and I know what happens in daycare centers.

Finally Ivy's friends arrived. It was a sunny afternoon and my work was done for the day. I had planned to run to the post office but was dragging my feet. Maybe she'd need me here to make cookies or pick up a pizza. She walked into the room. "So can you um, go out somewhere or something?" I didn't see the harm of my sitting in another room alone on the couch just in case, but the idea she didn't need me coupled with the fact she wanted that much privacy…it shows me she's really growing up and I've somehow transformed from mother to awkward roommate.

"I don't want any *That 70's Show* stuff going on," I said. I like to think she laughed but it was probably an eye roll. She's a good kid and I don't have to worry about her. I guess I never have.

It's the natural progression of things, this distance. I am at Starbucks for a little while, giving her time to miss me. Right.

Despite her age or independence or the fact that she does not need her stuffed animals anymore, or any of the childhood things she's outgrown, I will always think of her as my little girl.

From the time she was three until she was five and in kindergarten, she rode the train with me into Boston everyday to her daycare.

Even though that was a very unsure time in our lives, when we were beyond broke and I had no idea how our future would pan out, I have to say those were probably the best two years of my life. She was still little enough to carry and bundle under my coat when we walked in snowstorms through the North End. Maybe it was unhealthy that we ate out most nights at the train station because dinner at seven o'clock was too late for both of us, or that it was a rare day we didn't go to Mike's Pastry and buy something. It was a special time. And to this day I don't board the train without thinking of Ivy and our daily trips. I am perpetually proud of her.

When it's time for Ivy to go to college and move out, it's not going to be easy but it will be time. I will have California and Ryan waiting for me at the end of my journey and I am eagerly looking forward to that chapter of my life.

I hope that in years to come, whenever Ivy rides a train she thinks of me too.

I will keep her special dolls safe, just incase Ivy has brief lapses into childhood while she's spreading her wings.

Karma And Letting Go

May 2, 2012

When I was little my mother taught me that hating was bad, that it tarnished your soul and that it did no good. As a result, I made concessions for anyone who ever hurt me. "Well, it's not his fault, he was raised in an abusive family." Or "It's not her fault, she doesn't know better." That's all well and good but in a lot of ways, that set me up to be a doormat.

Somehow I made it through most of my life without realizing this. Until recently I thought my tolerance was an attribute. I got along with everyone, had few real enemies. Going through life with blinders on does wonders for you socially. I put up with a lot but never felt like I was compromising. When you set your mind to acceptance, you can justify just about any behavior. As I've grown older though I've gotten stronger. More willing to say no. You could call it jaded but I call it smart.

I'm sure to people who have known me forever, I've gone from Little Miss Sunshine to Little Miss Don't Even Think It. I don't know if it's because being with Ryan has empowered me, or I'm finally seeing people as they are, or if I'm just hyper aware now, overly cautious of someone corrupting the peace I've worked so hard to build and maintain.

I don't spend time hating anyone, but that's mainly because when I encounter a person who makes me miserable and hurts me, I bid them adieu. It's been my experience that when I do have to leave someone, sever an unhealthy friendship for example, they don't like it. Sometimes I can't help but feel like Frankenstein running from an angry mob.

"You come back here! How dare you! I'm not done with you!" But I walk away just the same. I don't retaliate or smear them on social networks. I just leave, peaceably. I figure somewhere along the line, they will get their just desert. Not from me. Maybe from Karma or God, or their consciences, or their children. Hard to say. Of Karma, Wikipedia says, "Followers of Buddhism and many followers of Hinduism consider the natural laws of causation sufficient to explain the effects of Karma."

Nelson Mandela has a great quote: "Resentment is like drinking poison and then hoping it will kill your enemies." There's another great quote from John F Kennedy. "Forgive your enemies but never forget their names." From those quotes, I think I'm on the right track. Forgive, don't dwell on hurt, but don't keep drinking from the same well that just made you sick. The "natural laws of causation" will fix it all up in the end.

I don't wish anyone harm. It's not my place to judge or punish. It's only my task to keep my own peace. I look back at my life a few years ago and see how many people have fallen by the wayside since then, people I've had to separate from. There have been a bunch. It wasn't easy but it was necessary.

Albert Einstein said, "I am not only a pacifist but a militant pacifist. I am willing to fight for peace."

It has been a fight. A lot of fights, clawing my way to peace, but I'm getting there.

I'm sitting home in the living room with the pets. Ivy is asleep. The house is silent. Silent as a mouse. It's serene.

When Love Turns
A Corner

May 27, 2012

Until a couple of weeks ago, all the times I've seen Ryan were on his turf, in his world.

Whenever I go to see him, there are no real life trappings around me. No dog, no cat, no teenage daughter, no house to clean, no food to cook. No snow. California is warm and sunny and pretty. It always feels like a long overdue vacation. If you've read my previous blogs, this whole relationship has been wonderfully romantic and magical.

Ryan has tried to stress to me the importance of my seeing it as it really is and I've argued that I AM seeing it that way, that my eyes are wide open.

But when Ryan came to visit Massachusetts a couple of weeks ago, in my world, it was a whole different experience.

It was his first time in Massachusetts and his first time on an airplane as a matter of fact. He took a red-eye flight in hopes he'd sleep through it and avoid the angst of flying. He barely slept at all. I picked him up at 8 AM at Logan Airport. He was pleasant but tired. We got back to my place and Henry and Lily immediately claimed him as their own. He sat on the couch, covered in mammals, and fell asleep.

He finally got to meet Ivy. In my mind, I suppose I was still looking to secure her a father, someone to look up to, to confide in. Ryan and I had often talked about how, despite our geographical distance, we were a family now. And I'd insert silently in my fairy tale mentality, "We'll live happily ever after." It's become apparent that Ivy is more realistic and grounded than I am when it comes to fantasy. She wants none of it. Now is now for her. No projecting, no pretending. She was pleasant to Ryan. There was no arguing but not much warmth either.

I've seen a few types of teens and how they react when their parents bring men or women home. There are the girls who will be pleasant and sweet and welcoming, and accept everyone without question. There are those who will hate whoever arrives, without discrimination or fairness. And then there are the Ivys. She's pretty much hated everyone I've met, in short order; but ultimately her instincts have proven true. Out of three kinds of kids, I'd prefer honesty and fair judgment even if it's just her opinion.

By Ryan's first night here, he got the sniffles which turned into a cold and fever. Over the next couple of days, he developed a cough. And then there was the issue of weather. It was supposed to be 60s and raining. But instead it was in the 80s and sunny, then 60s and rainy, then 70s and rainy. He got to see how we New Englanders live on a day-to-day basis. It was not like the California visits. Not by a long shot.

One night he woke up at 3AM coughing so badly he couldn't fall back asleep and ended up sleeping on the recliner. He woke me up around eight in the morning the next day. Ivy was at school. He sat and gave me the "We have to talk" look. I was afraid. I've had a few of those morning talks where someone wakes up and decides I'm too much. I was the Massachusetts Carly here. Scattered and busy and dripping with dependent mammals. He'd acted a little cool since he'd gotten here, more reserved. I felt like now that he'd seen this me, not the carefree California Carly, well I was more than he'd bargained for.

"You know, you're a lot more entrenched in this life than I realized," he said. "Moving out to California is going to be a much bigger deal than you realize. Letting go of all this. You've got a whole life here."

"Of course I do. I have an identity. I just want to be with you so I'll give this all up someday and move out there. It's okay." I'm not sure how it looked from his end, but for me, I felt everything flash before my eyes. This was surely his way of ending things, of letting me down easy. When he reads this blog, I'm sure he'll be surprised that I was going through all that, in my head, because it wasn't his intention.

He merely wanted me to start seeing everything for what it was. A real relationship with a future where it's not all heart and flowers. Where Ivy may never be thrilled with our relationship, where my relocating is going to rip my heart out, where one or both of us may sometimes be sick and not perky. I'm not sure why, but at first that realization rattled me. The voices of exes echoed in my brain, "You can't handle it when a relationship becomes real! As soon as the romance turns real you run!"

I looked to Ryan. In that moment, we turned a corner. It was hard corner for me. Like I was letting go of one stage to move onto the next. I was nervous the next couple of days, the rest of his visit. I was still on eggshells, on some level sure that he was moving toward a different step, of running himself. I couldn't be sure. I just knew I was afraid and it was another reminder of how much more he means to me than anyone else has.

But it was all fine. He went back home. I got some sleep, his cold got better. And we resumed our normal routine of nightly long phone calls and texts and emails and IMs during the day. But it's been different for me since then. It feels more secure and permanent. The veil of fantasy was lifted and I'm truly happy with the future that is underneath.

Here's to building a solid future—a real future.

Changing Vets

June 24, 2012

This blog started off comparing men to dogs. I suppose it's some-what gotten off course, as Ryan has shown me that not all men deserve that designation. Of course Ryan does love me unconditionally, is sweet and affectionate and is always happy to talk to and see me. I'm the same way with him. We're like two puppies. So maybe there is something to the dog analogy.

In keeping with the theme though, this week I did something I've wanted to do for years. I switched vets. I've had this veterinarian for ten years, and in that time, though she provides excellent medical care, she always makes me feel bad.

I understand there are those who will say that I allowed myself to feel bad, that it's on me. My ex-mother in law (the 2nd one) for example was always saying that if my ex chose to yell at me and tell me I was fat, and that made me sad, shame on me for caring what he said. I'd argue that he was my husband so of course I cared what he said. Water under the bridge though as I no longer speak to that ex-husband or his mother. And he no longer makes me feel sad. Back to the point though, my vet continually lectures me and disapproves of whatever I do when I visit. She also charges more than other vets in town.

If the cat gains weight, or loses weight, I get the look of disapproval. The folded arms. With my old dog, it was her chronic ear infections and later her Cushings Disease. The good doctor didn't blame me for the conditions but she always had the tone, and "the look." I've had other pets with her over the years and though the animals get their shots on time and are in good health, I always walk out of her office feeling like crap. The vet has the same power over me Husband # 2 did. Logically, I know her crankiness is on her because I AM a good pet owner and damn it, I WAS a good wife. But it's hurtful nonetheless.

Shame on me for staying with both of them as long as I did. I left the husband five years ago but the vet...well this week I made the break.

I found a new one, referred by a friend. I called and explained that the old doctor charged a lot and wasn't very nice. The new vet understood and promised that things would be different now. Much like Ryan did when we first started talking. "Things are going to change for you."

It took me two hours of angst before I got up the nerve to call the old vet to fax over the records. I was ready for a fight but said evenly, "I'm getting Lily spayed somewhere else, can you fax over her records?" I couldn't help but recall a similar situation five years ago when I had reached my mean limit with the ex and I said something along the lines of, "You need to call a bank to buy me out. I'm going to look at a new house. I'm done."

It's funny what the last straw will be. With the vet it was a lecture about heartworm medicine. With the ex it was my strolling across the room feeling thinner than I ever had and having him say,"I can't understand how you think THIS is your ideal weight." With all the problems over the years, it was his taking the wind out of my sails that final time that ended it.

The vet conceded, as did the ex. She has plenty of other patients and he has a new wife. We're all better off.

I realized today that my affiliation with the doctor was the last unhealthy relationship I had left in my life. When I look back to a year ago and the people I hung out with all the time and called friends, I'm bewildered. That ex was one of them. Why did I surround myself with people who made me feel bad and frustrated me? I don't really know. Habit? Not knowing there was another way? Not realizing that if I broke out of that circle there would be a better pack to welcome me?

There are less dogs around me now but the ones that are here are awesome. Happy dogs with good temperaments and tails that wag all the time.

I am a happy puppy.

Learning To Walk Again

July 4, 2012

I'm on a JetBlue airplane on the way home from California, after spending several days with Ryan. Each time I visit, it gets harder to leave. This trip out was our fifth time seeing each other. We talked about that this weekend, how it's funny we've really only had five dates, yet we feel like we've always been together. Or always should have been.

Of course each date lasts several days, so that helps. And there are those hours-long phone calls every single night for eight straight months. There would be volumes of emails and texts, if you were to compile them all in one place. Each word and minute has sparked a new facet of connection, forged another level of closeness.

This trip he took me to Disneyland. I've been to Disney World a few times. None of the trips were all that fun as I was constantly arguing with Husband # 2. Even though Ivy was with me and it's supposedly the most fun place on earth, I was so rigid and resentful and cranky, it wasn't fun for me. In my defense, being yelled at for not doing my nails, or for not being all decked out in heels like Peg Bundy for our five A.M. flights tended to set those past trips off on a bad start. Plus honestly who doesn't want to buy special treats from the bakeries on Main Street? Look but don't touch is not a good motto for the Disney theme parks.

So here was Ryan setting out to show me the correct way to enjoy "his" Disney. The thing that's remarkable about Ryan, or rather how I am with Ryan, is that I see everything through different eyes than I have with anyone else. Maybe it's because I know he has my back so I can relax and enjoy his company, or because he encourages my sense of whimsy. Whatever the reason, things are always nice.

As we drove to the park, I was so excited. I couldn't wait to get there. And once we walked in, all the rides called to me. I couldn't wait to drink it all in, to experience this "fun" that everyone else gets out of the Disney parks. I know a bunch of adults without children, or with children who have grown, who spend what I used to think was a disproportionate amount of time in Orlando or Anaheim. But now I get it. Finally. It is the most fun place on earth. How did I miss that?

As I was walking through Toontown I texted Ivy and told her we simply had to come back here for Christmas vacation. I told her I was having FUN. She surely knows what a coup that is. "There's not much of your childhood left," I typed to her. That reality is an albatross around my neck. Soon she will be grown. How sad if she never gets to experience the light hearted me I am when I'm around Ryan.

I feel badly I've been uptight for so long, but things just turned out that way. Being a single mother for most of the last sixteen years made it tough to let go and just relax and be giddy. I tried, really I did. But being both parents and hence compensating, and juggling bills, and trying to do everything differently for her than I ever had, trying and failing to find her a good father figure . . . well, I don't know if there's any way I could have relaxed before now given my circumstances.

But it's not too late now. Sometimes when I'm with Ryan, I feel like someone who is recovering from a major car accident or stroke and just learning to walk all over again, or recognize the feel of an orange or the name of a song. "And now take another step forward," he says. "I'm here for you." This Carly is so much stronger on my feet, so much more grateful for each new (or revisited) sight and sound and sensation.

Having someone to lean on, trusting he will hold me up if I falter as I'm finding my way, makes all the difference in rediscovery and in life.

Baby steps to happiness.

Greeting Cards From Exes

July 22, 2012

Last week I decided to sort through a box labeled "Special Cards." I'm trying to whittle down my belongings to what I need, things that matter. For years I've thrown every greeting card in that box and it's unlikely I need them all.

I brought the box up from the basement and started reading through the cards. Some were special, from Ivy, Ryan, or relatives. There were also a whole bunch from exes. If the current Me received those cards, I would have walked away. Reading between the lines were commitment issues and fear of intimacy.

There was a Valentine's Day card from one particular guy, Husband # 2. On the outside it said, "I lo-, I lo-" and on the inside, "I like you a lot." I read it and wondered why he even put the love idea out there. Why not just buy me a card that said, "You're special." It reminded me of the time we later went engagement ring shopping. We drove there together and he picked one out that was much larger that I had expected. I was thrilled of course because it was a lovely ring and this proposal was a long time coming. I'd told people we were going out that night, for that very reason. Ivy's daycare lady kept her a couple of extra hours for the occasion. But at the store he told the man he wasn't ready to buy one after all. I found out later he'd snuck out and bought it to put away for when HE was ready. In those months that lapsed until he gave it to me though I was hurt, unnecessarily, kind of like with the card. "I lo-, I lo-…I like you." The whole relationship followed that pattern, of dangling the love carrot only to withdraw it.

There were cards from two serious boyfriends I had after him, and I laughed (in a sad way) when I read them. Every card, somewhere in the body, had "sorry" printed in apologetic cursive. Another thing I noticed was for the holiday cards, from both men, they read, "I hope next (Valentine's Day, Christmas, etc.) year we're still together." Okay fine, we weren't still together, but looking back, the fact that all the cards had apologies and foreshadowed a potential break up should have been big red flags. I know people make mistakes and hurt each other, but shouldn't apologies be a rarity and not the norm? There were no, "Just because I love you," cards in the box. What was I thinking?

I remember being in relationships over the years and standing in the card section, struggling to find a card that said what I needed it to. "I don't want to be here," "Trying to extricate myself from…" "Can we start over? Alone?" Buying cards is a lot easier now. I actually pick them up quite often to send to Ryan because I love that I can go in the romance section and pick up any one and the mushy sentiments ring true.

By the way, I threw away all the cards except the ones from Ivy, Ryan and family. Like my new life, this box contains nothing but happiness and hope.

Feeling Grown Up

August 29, 2012

Ivy got her license a few weeks ago. It's the newest in a list of milestones I've witnessed in the last few years. But this was a big one.

I take a train to work and used to drive a mile and pay four dollars a day to park. Since she got her license I started walking to the train, and she picks me up at the end of the day. The first evening she rolled into the station in my car she was smiling broadly. At her age, she seems always to be playing it cool around me. Either rolling her eyes or saying I'm awkward, unless I catch her in an unguarded happy or giddy moment.

That first day I got in, she was smiling ear to ear. She said, "I drove this morning and there was nothing on but talk radio so I listened to it and felt so grown up." I knew what she meant because one of the fun things about milestones is that you suddenly feel different. You can tell some part of you has changed and there's no going back. You are independent in a way you weren't before, and your childhood sloughs off one layer at a time.

I did a lot of growing up all at once when I was about eighteen. I have a September birthday so right before I should have gone away to college, I decided against it. There I was, seventeen with no idea how to do anything, no license, no car. I scrambled, took two road lessons borrowing the driving school's car, got my permit, then license. I immediately applied for a job, of all places, at a rental car company where I'd be driving all the time. I moved out of my house about a month after I turned eighteen.

I had a boyfriend for a while and we got a place. I spent my days trying to make it a home, learning to cook, playing house. I got a checking account and even learned to crochet. I was an adult with a full-time job, an apartment, a boyfriend...When that ended not too long after (because in retrospect I was still a child), I got my own place. I was starting from scratch again and it was scary but it was also pretty fun. I was even more mature than before because I was taking care of myself. I got a promotion and ran an office, had a company car. Like my daughter, I felt so grown up.

I got another job a couple of years later where I had to dress up every day. It was thrilling. I still felt like an impostor, like a teen playing office. It also felt a lot like high school because they were cliques there and mean people and nerds. That job lasted only six months because I got yelled at by clients all the time and can't handle anger. Ah the joys of working in the payables department of a company with no money.

But then I got a job in Boston. A real job. I got credit cards and a brand-new car. I parked it each day and took a bus into the city and really had to dress up. Skirts and heels and jewelry. I turned twenty-one eventually, then met someone and got married and years later had a baby.

And somewhere in there I stopped feeling so grown up and just saw this is the way things were. The thrill kind of wore off. I'm guessing it happened in a murky bunch of years when I gradually went from playing house to becoming a full-fledged adult. I stopped appreciating the freedom that being an adult gives you.

Hearing my daughter say those words brought it all back.

Reflecting on it, despite the mammoth responsibility that adulthood brings, it's really cool that I can just jump in the car and go to the store and buy things to make dinner. I can use my washer and dryer to clean my clothes, and use my grown up vacuum and dishwasher to help me along. I can stay up later than I know is good for me and be tired the next day and relish the exhaustion because it's my doing.

I haven't been a child in a very long time, but seeing Ivy slowly emerge from hers reminds that indeed, it's really cool to be a grown up.

Rainy Days
October 14, 2012

A year ago I couldn't stop talking to everyone who would listen about this guy from California who I was just friends with, but whose emails brightened my day. He'd become my new best friend even though we hadn't met. My pals saw through it. A week later he and I cemented things, moved to phone calls, and conceded that indeed we were destined for something much bigger. It's been a romantic whirlwind of fun and happiness.

About a month ago I ran into a woman I hadn't seen in some time and updated her about Ryan, and our long distance relationship. She said, "Isn't that really hard, only seeing him every couple of months?" I replied that no, it was fine. It was all we knew so it was manageable, sometimes lonelier than others, but overall not so bad.

I need to retract that now. Missing him has suddenly become difficult, every single day. The fact we've had almost twenty straight days of gray skies and/or rain since he left doesn't help.

I believe his last visit caused this new closeness and hence this melancholy.

Ryan came out for a visit three weeks ago. On its surface it was like all our visits, where we visited tourist hot spots and ate out a lot. This time though we spent a whole week together here in Massachusetts. It's always harder when he comes here because there are the trappings of my everyday life that aren't present in Simi Valley.

This time for example I had to work one of the days for an end of the month crunch. I worked from my room, pets at my side, radio blasting. Ryan was on his own and I was in get-something-done mode.

I remained locked in that hyperactive mode for most of the visit. I confess I'm like that a good portion of the time. Ryan is thankfully more laid back. I also had a ton of homework for an accounting class I am taking so was overwhelmed and spent too much time hovering over my textbook, utterly confused.

In addition, I didn't get enough sleep for most of the trip because Ryan needs less than I do. I was hoping he'd feel the time difference and sleep till a normal hour. But no, he was up at 6 AM bright-eyed and bushy-tailed. I was not. To say I was cranky was probably an understatement.

We also dealt with car conflict and teenage angst more than I would have liked. Ivy now has her license and usually drops me at the train station and takes the car to school for the day. We needed transportation so she had to take the school bus.

From a pet standpoint, Lily was her messy, restless puppy self. "When I was young and had a dog…" Ryan said, and regaled me with how dogs used to be housebroken and blahblahblah.

Ryan decided to start a publishing company featuring me as his main and only author until he gets up and running and takes on more clients. In the past months he'd created some terrific book covers for stories I've put up on Kindle. But now we're working on my first adult novel. It's a suspense thriller and I'm quite excited. He read it on the day I had to work. He liked it. Good. He pointed out a few small things. Also good, and helpful. But I'm a writer and hypersensitive so valid or not, every criticism stings a little until I work through it, fix it, and get praise again. We went back and forth on some minor corrections which showed me a dynamic with him I hadn't seen before.

The week was more real than all the other visits. We got on each other's nerves a bit but it felt natural and comfortable. When I dropped him off at the airport all I could think of was how tired I was. But then after a nice long nap, all I could think of was how much I missed him.

I'm going out there early November which is a relief because I think this year, more than any other, the gray skies and daily rain are getting to me. I need some sunshine and need to see Ryan again.

Weddings And Wishes

October 27, 2012

I went to a wedding tonight and was touched when the bride walked down the aisle toward her future husband. Until that moment though, as I looked around the room at the decorations and the cake, the place settings, centerpieces, the guest book and all the other things required to put a wedding together, I cringed.

I've had two weddings already. The first was in Jamaica to Ivy's Dad. I wanted to forego a wedding because I was intimidated by the process. But then I felt guilty that no one could celebrate or publicly acknowledge our nuptials. So though we were married on a beach far away in the company of strangers, I still put together a reception with about a hundred people when we returned home. We were very young and on an extremely limited budget. I recall buying flowers from a Haymarket type vendor in Boston the day before, and vases from the Christmas Tree Shop. We hired a caterer who made meatballs and pasta at $6.50 a person. All I remember about that night was how stressful it was to prepare everything. On the way home my ex and I fought like crazy. I remember thinking I had made a mistake. All that work for nothing.

We chugged on for eight years and eventually, through circumstances we couldn't fix, split up.

When I later married the second time, I wanted a big and real wedding in a mansion, with a limo and real dress (not beach attire). We were in a better financial position than when I was a kid. But he said no. I wanted to honeymoon in Costa Rica. He said no. He wanted a beach honeymoon. In the end we had a micro wedding in a restaurant with about thirty people and a honeymoon on a beach.

My mother drove me so I could show up separately, still clinging to some sense of tradition. I almost threw up in the driveway and I couldn't stop shaking. I kept thinking Why am I doing this? Is it too late to change my mind? That wedding didn't involve as much planning but it was by no means fun. I didn't look at my new groom with love and gratitude. I just watched him watch me, keeping me at arms' length. When we got home I tore my dress on a nail. I said it was a shame because I liked the dress. All he could say was something like "Too bad you didn't lose the weight." Yeah, big mistake on my part. We honeymooned on an island far away and were divorced 18 months later. I had learned to cut my losses.

And I've been pretty marriage resistant since. A few years ago someone asked me if I wanted to marry Mr. X (long gone) and I said "God no!" Once I said it out loud I wondered what I was doing with someone whose involvement would cause a reaction like that.

I've been happily legally single the last five years but lately I'm thinking that with Ryan, it would be nice to try again. When I saw the bride and groom tonight smile at each other, I could see love and innocence and respect. I didn't see angst about the planning, or the traffic that caused some people to be late, or the upcoming hurricane that caused some people to cancel. I didn't see a bride whose face was filled with regret, or a groom who was detached.

I saw two people legally and emotionally becoming one, in front of everyone. Though the room was full, they were alone. Just the two of them, smiling and happy.

Someday, with Ryan, that's the kind of wedding I want. (hypothetically, I mean, we're not engaged). It doesn't matter to me if there are 100 people in a hall or just a few of us in an Elvis Chapel in Vegas. No matter the venue or the amount of guests, I know it'll just be the two of us in our hearts and in the room, finally getting it right.

Here's to weddings and wishes.

When You Run Into An Ex

November 25, 2012

Thanksgiving has passed and Christmas is just around the corner. It's been a long rough year but the holiday spirit always makes me feel warm and happy. I won't see Ryan over the holidays because he's out of vacation days. But time is just time and it will go by quickly as it always does. For now though, his virtual presence is enough to make the holidays brighter.

If you read my older blogs, from almost a year ago, I spoke about Husband #2. When I started the Carly blog we were best friends, despite how bad our short marriage had been. He went above and beyond as a friend to make up for everything. He had a nice fiancé that was better suited to him that I had been. And I had "met" Ryan and was very happy. We had started to cool off the friendship because we were both with other people and they were the ones we should have been focusing on. But it was still nice knowing he was there if I needed anything. Okay, looking back it was pretty dysfunctional but it was comfortable.

And then I had a dismantling with a mutual friend of ours and suddenly our friendship was over. There was no argument. He just stopped calling and he blocked me on Facebook. It was hurtful and I was confused. I could have reached out but there was no point. It was time to move on.

I had Ryan. And honestly, it did make it easier not to be around someone I had chosen to leave. It was nice to focus solely on Ryan and our relationship, and never look back. Though I live in a very small town and the ex lives just a mile from me, I've never run into him.

Today though I was headed into the grocery store and saw him walk in. It's been almost a year since we've spoken and so I grew anxious. I waited in my car for him to leave so I could avoid speaking to him. Let sleeping dogs lie.

But then I remembered that I wanted to tell him about Ivy, about some problems she's had, about her successes. He was in our lives for seven years and there were things he should know, things I would have told him if hadn't pulled away. And honestly, the tension of always worrying I'd run into him and how it would go makes me uncomfortable. So I got out of the car and went inside, not intent on finding him but figuring if I saw him, then so be it.

I did. In the bread aisle. It was weird. He looked shocked and upset to see me. He said, "Oh. Hi." We had a solid wall between us, or we may as well have. I am nothing if not confrontational so I asked calmly, "So how come you just stopped talking to us a year ago?" He explained why, which was the reason I suspected. We had an awkward few minutes of updates: My new book, his wife's new business, Ryan. I filled him in on some Ivy stuff.

The conversation was superficial and cold. It reminded me how the relationship had been. We had been an awful match. Had never truly bonded. There was no drama now. Just cool, calm talking, a relaying of facts. Like we had a really bad date we wanted to forget, but saw each other and had to make an effort to make it less awkward than it was.

In the end he said his wife was waiting in the car and he had to go, and maybe he'd run into me in the store again someday.

I said Merry Christmas and he said Happy Thanksgiving. He left and I wandered the store and bought groceries. Seeing him rattled me a little. I guess the coldness threw me. It wasn't cruel coldness, like anger. There was just nothing.

It was an enlightening visit to the grocery store. I went there to buy ingredients for lasagna and meatballs and left with a feeling of emptiness but a trove of closure.

To leaving the past in the past.

Milestones

December 6, 2012

About a year ago I met Ryan in person for the first time. We'd spoken for several months on the phone and online and I'd emotionally already pledged my heart to him. I looked to our physical meeting as a mere formality. My friends didn't see it that way. Nor did my family. To them, it started when we met. Before that, anything could happen.

I've been watching this show *Catfish* the last few weeks. The idea is based on a documentary (by the same name) a man had made about a long distance relationship he had, and the shocking first meeting of the woman he'd come to love. Now he puts people together who haven't yet met but have fallen totally in love. I thought it might be a cool inspiring show but instead, all these meetings are horrific. Of the three I've watched, all from the girls' angle waiting to meet the men, their matches were disturbing.

All three of these couples had talked about love and marriage and commitment before they ever met. Just like Ryan and I. Two of the three episodes featured Mr. Right as…insane women. Yes, that's right. Women. Last week's episode featured a girl's Mr. Right after almost a year of communicating. Mr. Right was not a twenty-seven year old exotic dancer with two kids but a thirty-two year old guy (I think he was really older) with four kids. And he did not have a dancer body. Not to mention the fake name and profile.

I mention these scenarios because I see better now why everyone was so worried about my meeting Ryan for the first time. For one, I'd met some weirdos online, and in real life for that matter. And two, Ryan lived on the other side of the country. How could it go well? And even if it did, who would move?

The panic I felt last December though was the worry that we wouldn't click, or he'd be a jerk to wait staff or to me, or be condescending or any of a number of things I'd experienced up till that point in my unsuccessful relationship history. But as you all know from subsequent blogs, it was fine. Just fine.

Now that a whole year has gone by since our first meeting, I'm thinking everyone who was worried is feeling better now.

To date, we've met most of each other's friends, I've met some of his family, he's met Ivy, twice. Seven in person visits, one birthday each, rounding to our second Christmas. More phone calls, emails, texts and IMs that I've ever shared with anyone. He's been there for me, every step I've taken all year.

Things are good in Carly/Ryan land. Online relationships don't always work out. But ours sure did.

One More Christmas After This

December 23, 2012

Last Christmas was the first one I shared with Ryan. We didn't experience it in person, as we only met in real life early December, and two trips across the country in a month wasn't a possibility. We opened our presents together over the phone. He picked all wonderful gifts which showed even in the few months we'd gotten to know each other, that he truly understood me. We knew then it would be the last holiday we'd spend apart.

But this Christmas is in two days and there's no chance of us being together. The reality of the cost of flying back and forth and of limited vacation time factors in. We saw each other in November and now have a long stretch until February. So like last year I've got a bunch of presents from him that are sitting on my table waiting until Christmas Eve to be unwrapped. And he's got some that I sent with much love.

It's true we've spent more time apart than together in 2011 and 2012 but we're still just as emotionally connected as ever. Sometimes I get busy at work and don't think much about the relationship. Then suddenly I'll remember that there's someone out there whose presence has changed my life.

I am reminded that just one more Christmas after this and the week-long stretches of gray rainy days and damp air will give way to sunshine and palm trees and a whole different ocean. I am reminded that in less two years I won't be a single parent anymore and someone will be there to watch over me, to literally (not virtually) stand by my side and help me in life.

I sit alone tonight thinking that just one more Christmas after this one and Ryan and I really will spend all the holidays together. I've baked all afternoon for family gatherings. All my gifts for everyone are wrapped. Ivy is out with friends. The tree is lit, and now it's time to just sit and wait.

My life has become a continual emotional conflict. On the one hand, I can't wait to start my life with Ryan, to move to California. They say you can't run away from things, and that's true. But you can leave towns and areas where baggage is piled up all around you like rotted trash. You can dream of living in a place where nothing is familiar, where nothing is cursed, and you don't have to worry about running into someone you never ever wanted to see again.

On the flip side, once Ivy graduates from high school, this part of our lives is over. I'll still be her mother of course, but the 0-18 years part of her life will have passed. She'll be well on her way to adulthood, and long gone will be the days when she sat on my feet when I walked, or held my hand, or trusted I had the answers to everything.

One more Christmas after this and it won't just be Ivy and me anymore, sitting here with the pets watching our favorite movies over and over again. She'll be at college and gradually starting a life of her own. And there will be another person in our family. Well one more person and his turtle. Can't forget Tortuga.

It's been a long hard year. And of all the years since Ivy was born, since it's been just the two of us, none drove home testing the difficulties of raising a child alone like this one has. If Ryan hadn't entered my life, even if it is mostly virtual, I don't know how well I would have fared. There's a limit to everyone's strength and mine was tested.

So on this eve of Christmas eve, I am relieved that it's just one more Christmas after this until the next stage of all our lives start.

I wish everyone a happy holiday and a new year filled with hope and celebration for good things to come.

Putting Down Roots

January 27, 2013

I was at work the other day talking to a coworker about my future relocation to California. She asked the valid question, "What if you move and it doesn't work out? You'll be stuck out there." She's not the first person to ask it. In other situations, that same thought would be crossing my mind on a daily basis.

I replied simply that, "Nothing will happen." But even if it did, like if Ryan died which I can see as the only thing that would prevent a long future together, California is eventually going to be my new home.

When I was in high school, I'd readied myself to go to Salem State College. I'd planned, and dreamed, and breathed in the ocean air, mentally preparing myself for this new life. I ended up not going last minute (something I regret to this day) and stayed in my home town. Eventually I met my first husband and we moved around quite a bit, all within a thirty mile radius. Each new town I made my own, the best I could.

I loved Middleboro. It was by far the cutest town I've ever lived in. I lived there for about five years. I never got to know any of my neighbors well, and didn't socialize much, but that town ... I walked to the Boston bus for years, in front of the town hall. The church was there, and Ivy's kindergarten. Each summer I'd walk down the street to the local fair and watch fireworks. If it weren't for the life troubles at the time, it would have been Heaven. In some ways I guess it still was. I loved the cranberry bogs and flat land and the undeniable charm around every corner.

After the divorce I moved ninety miles north to where I live now, on the New Hampshire border. It was for a man and I knew nothing about the town except that he lived there. It was scary and hard, but I was excited for the adventure. The relationship didn't work out, and now we are strangers, but this has become my town, as if I was born here. The hills, and winding roads without streets signs, and the ski lodge, and the river that runs through all the local towns have become my mental backdrop to life.

So when I think of Simi Valley, I am mixed with fear of moving to a new place, but excitement over settling in to another life, one that will eventually become my own, as if I was born there. This time it's different because I feel truly connected to many people here, relatives and friends, and even just the sights in the town. And sometimes I worry that I'll never see another town that looks like this one again. But one time Ryan drove me to Ojai and that was a darn cute little village. I wouldn't live there (too far from work) but it's drivable.

As much as I've grown to love the duck pond near my house, shining in the spring, reflecting leaves in the fall, or frozen over in winter, I will learn to love the orange groves, staffed with migrant farm workers. I'll learn to love the palm trees the way I love the pines. And the mountains, well they are already a part of Ventura County that take my breath away.

I know this blog doesn't touch much upon my love for Ryan. That's evident by now. But this is more about the other side of relocation. Forging a connection, nesting in the new place, while missing the other one. I'll miss the sound of plows overnight, and dog prints in the snow, but I won't miss the cold, or spending all my nights and weekends alone. And trust me, there is something intoxicating about standing outside in shorts and a tank top at 8 AM and feeling warmth on my skin, and finding lizards in the closet.

For now, I visit as much as I can, and I've sent a few things on ahead, moving in a handful of items at a time. I've sent a jar of rain and some acorns, some fall leaves. With my next box I'll send pinecones and (melted) snow. Little by little I'll make it my home. Ivy will be in college, hopefully not too far away in San Diego. Part of me thinks this is just like when she was six and we moved north, where I drove us toward a new life, car filled with our things and pets, toward an adventure. I guess it's somewhat the same (though she'll be eighteen and a half), pulling us both from what we know to start fresh. College and adulthood and a world so different from what we've known.

It's all still a ways off, another eighteen months or so, but it's on my mind, as Ivy grows older, SATs loom in the near future, and time rushes faster than I can track it. Each time I drive down the street I capture images in my head. Each time I meet with local friends or take the subway, I'm logging it all in.

Nothing bad will happen, and California is my future. But New England will always run in my blood.

Grabbing The Brass Ring

February 12, 2013

I've been around the bend a few times, had my share of figurative carousel rides through hell, starting and ending at the same place and pretty much repeating the same pattern until I grew nauseous and tired. All those times though, what kept me going was the quest for that brass ring. I was always so close to utter happiness, peace, and a permanent loving relationship. But then whoosh, I'd miss it. Again.

For anyone who's been following this blog since July of 2011, you know that I finally caught the ring. In two days I'll be flying to L.A. to see Ryan again. Generally we mail packages and letters back and forth, and seeing each other in real life on holidays doesn't work out. But this year I will see him on Valentine's Day. We're both excited about this, since this holiday is all about love and it's just not the same from 3000 miles away.

I have a friend who just started dating someone. They are going through the brand-new thrilling part filled with excitement, and insecurity, and breathlessness. I hope it works out for her and him as love, if you can partner up with someone worthy and compatible, is wonderful. Some people think that is the brass ring: The out-of-your-mind-thrill of new love, when you think about that special someone constantly, and mess up your work, and can't sleep, or eat. But to me, that stage is just the carousel ride. It's fun and filled with hope, and dizzying. But that's just the ride, what you do to get "there."

To me, the brass ring is where I am now with Ryan. The easy, quiet comfortableness. It's exciting too, but even better is the feeling that he's always right here next to me (even though of course he's physically not). He's the first person I call with news, my best friend. I think about him all the time, but it's more an awareness than thought. Not conscious. We have an understanding. That's the brass ring.

Imagine if kids knew that grabbing the brass ring would grant them the gift of getting off the wild ride and onto something akin to life on a really comfy couch hugging your favorite Teddy Bear. I know plenty of adults who would rather keep riding, continuing the thrill of new love. But to me, comfy and cozy is about the best prize I could ever get.

Happy almost Valentine's Day to everyone in all the stages of love, those who have loved and lost, who are waiting to meet the one, and to those who have grabbed their brass ring.

Finding New England On The West Coast

February 25, 2013

I went to Building 19 the other night in search of a cheap picture to hang in my hallway since I did some decor reshuffling. Whenever I visit that store, I experience quite a bit of nostalgia. One of the reasons is because I used to go with my grandparents when I was a kid, but it's also because nothing has changed in that store. Nothing.

The location I used to visit was in southern Massachusetts, or maybe RI, but they are the same. Literally, they probably have all the original fixtures and chairs and recycled carriages from the 1970s. There's something refreshing about going somewhere that is frozen in time, in a world that changes so fast it's dizzying.

That might be one of the biggest draws of New England to me, the oldness and steadiness of it. As I browsed the cheap dusty paintings in the store, and walked on the old and somewhat dirty linoleum, I saw a few prints that caught me off guard. They were of typical New England farmhouses and barns in different seasons. One was a weathered white house next to a snowy tree. Another was an antique red barn next to a tractor. The trees were filled with bright fall leaves, and a few had fallen to the ground. I got choked up thinking that once I was in CA, I wouldn't be likely to see scenes like this in real life anymore.

I couldn't buy the pictures, didn't want the reminder of what I'd be leaving.

When I got home though, I started thinking about the trip I'd just returned from, the Valentine's Day visit to California. During my trip there, except for being mesmerized by the scenic views of the mountains and valleys and ocean, it didn't feel like I was somewhere else. I felt very at home there, not like I was an Eastern impostor.

This was the visit where I crossed over into forgetting I was somewhere else. Over time I have accumulated more stuff at Ryan's house. The first night I put on my happy bunny flannel PJ pants and t-shirt and fuzzy socks. Just like home. One day we drove up to Santa Barbara. It was breathtaking but in a way looked a lot like New England, like Rockport or Freeport. It even smelled the same: Cotton candy, salt water, and fried fish. The pier was weathered and the seagulls overhead could have been cousins of the ones who hang out at our Building 19.

Admittedly the fish and chips were prepared in a healthier breading and the fries weren't shiny with grease. And the coleslaw didn't have a mayonnaise base. But the view was the same from my window seat.

After that we went up to see friends who were camping up at Lake Chumash. The campground was up a very windy and high mountain road. When we got to their site, I was greeted with familiar (Simi Valley) faces. And from up there, it felt just like New England. Tall trees, leaves, some pine, water below, dark dirt beneath our feet. It was cool enough by five o'clock that I had to put on my flannel shirt. Not so different after all.

Today I was cleaning out the last jar of my strawberry preserves. The strawberries in stores here now are small and sour and hard. I thought happily of when I'm in CA and can make fresh jam any time I want, not just during the very short harvest season.

Most of the places I've lived in have had brick or at least brick front construction. I suppose there's no getting around that out in earthquake country, but the rest I think I can replicate. Maybe the outside of the house will be stucco with those funny clay roof tiles but the inside of our place can be cozy and filled with New England charm.

And maybe out there I'll be more tan, and thinner, because I won't be able to hide in big heavy sweaters and corduroys and South Park parkas for most of the year, but inside I will still be cozy. I'll still make comfort foods, and will can things, and use flannel sheets, even if we have to turn the AC on really high.

There's a little New England everywhere you go, and I think it will all work out just fine.

Dreaming In English

March 3, 2013

Each week, I meet with a man from Jordan and help him to speak and understand English better. He's got a good command of the language but still needs help with conversation and writing. I've asked him a couple of times if he dreams in English yet. It's been said that once you start dreaming in your new language, it has become a part of you.

I had a dream two nights ago that Ryan and I were dropping Ivy off at college for the first time. She ran off with some new friends and quickly disappeared. I sat in an auditorium where a lecturer told us what to expect for our kids. Ryan wasn't there then, it was just me and a bunch of strangers. Like me, the other parents showed a mix of excitement and sadness.

I started crying then and rushed outside, unable to cope with the idea that Ivy was moving on from childhood. I ran through the heavily wooded campus (which I thought was odd for San Diego). On the other side, my left, were buildings. Suddenly I came to a small cafe and found Ryan sitting at a table reading. He has bad knees even in real life and sometimes he sits things out. He looked up then ran over and hugged and consoled me. I don't remember much else except that he was there for me and made everything okay.

When Ryan and I first started dating, I never dreamt about him. I dreamt about Ivy and me, situations we'd find ourselves in. I dreamt about work and relatives and friends. Having a virtual relationship made it hard for Ryan to begin existence in my subconscious. I wanted to dream about him. I read emails from him and we talked on the phone for hours each night. And I'd visit him whenever I could. But like the man I'm tutoring in English, I was unable to fully incorporate Ryan into my mind. Reading and conversation only take you so far, and it's a slower process than when you're fully immersed in a situation.

Last night I had another dream about Ryan. This time he had picked out a house for all of us to live in. I was angry that we were going to sign papers on a place he had never actually seen. He assured me it was fine and he found us just the right place. I spent most of the dream sitting in a law office with Ivy and him, trying to search the address on my computer so I could see pictures of it, read about the amenities and details, so I'd know the house was livable. But my computer kept freezing. And no matter what I typed, the computer kept auto filling with invalid web addresses.

Ryan emerged from an office and told me the closing would be delayed a few hours. So we all got in the car. I had finally discovered the name of the complex on a closing document so set my GPS and kept searching on my computer—somehow as I drove. Before any of the technology worked, I looked up and saw a huge luxury complex. A wrought iron gate greeted us with the letter F, for a place called Fairhaven Gardens.

The place was spectacular. Huge and airy and bigger than a condo would be in real life. Bright shiny sun and swimming pools. It was more like a resort on a tropical island. Ryan knew a woman who lived there so she gave us a tour of her place which she said would be just like ours. I noticed then there were no dogs running around and I worried that Ryan had forgotten we needed a place that allowed pets. Then I looked at the neighbor's yard (we all had huge private grassy patios) and saw a big black lab puppy. I was relieved, and reprimanded myself for thinking that Ryan would ever fail me.

Okay so I know these are just dreams but they really say something about where my head is. For one, Ryan is always around. Not in real life. The most I see him is every two months. But at night, he's always there, rescuing me, or hanging around to make sure I'm okay.

In terms of my relationship with Ryan, I think it's safe to say I'm finally dreaming in English.

The Curve Ball

March 5, 2013

At my age, I like to think I'm an adult. I'm in control of my emotions and my life is pretty settled and happy. I've got my share of stress like anyone: typical parenting stuff, financial challenges, family discord on occasion. But overall, things are finally just right. Predictable and manageable. Even Lily the puppy has settled into an easy routine. No surprises.

But a couple of weeks ago I got an unexpected email from my stepfather and suddenly I felt like a little girl again. I have to wonder if any woman, no matter her age or place in life ever loses that inner child. For anyone who has been reading this blog all along, or knows me in real life, you'll know I haven't seen this man in over twenty years. He hasn't met Ivy, and except for a couple of emails or calls in all these years, we've had no contact.

Even so, he was the man who raised me, was there for all the years of my early and late childhood. He left when I was thirteen, the summer before high school. Legally I suppose he's my ex-stepfather but I never accepted that he was gone forever. He never called me a stepchild. "This is my daughter, Carly," he'd say. And I'd beam with pride. His email said he's been reading my blog and following my life online for some time.

Life would have been easier if he had stayed of course; and I could be a true childish brat and blame his absence for everything bad that ever happened in my life. But realistically more damage was done by the people in my life than those out if it. He was only thirty-three when he left a difficult marriage and two stepchildren aged thirteen and eighteen years old. He still visited me for years. It wasn't cold turkey but a gradual parting between us, as I grew up.

He was only twenty-three or so when we "got him" and I remember clearly those first visits. Almost immediately he jumped in with both feet and we had a full family (for a while). Ten years is a long time in the life of a little girl, and though he left before I was an adult, he was a huge influence on me. When I was in kindergarten he went to Panama for the National Guard. I'm not sure how long he was gone but he brought me home a doll, which I named Panama and kept for many, many years.

I've written ad nauseam in this blog about all that was wrong in my past, and how hard everything was, and how strong my struggles made me. But for tonight I want to remember some wonderful parts of my childhood, times when my "dad" was still around full time.

We are planning to meet again soon. Twenty years is a long time, but oddly enough I don't feel any older than I did then, or any different. It certainly didn't feel like it was that long ago we all split up and moved our separate ways. For better or worse, he and I both turned out all right in the end and seemingly for all we've both endured, we're the same underneath.

With all that's happened in the past years, it's nice this has come full circle. Years ago I was at a marriage counselor and told the doctor about my step-dad and how we hadn't spoken but I was sure he still thought of me, that he still cared even if he wasn't there. The doctor looked at me seriously and said, "You need to accept that he was just your stepfather and he's moved on. He has no obligation to you. What if he doesn't care?" I argued that he did. The doctor looked at me like I was a foolish little girl. "You need to let him go."

It was fair advice but I am glad that I will get to see my stepfather again after all, through the eyes of an adult, to see just how much little girl is still left inside.

Catharsis

March 10, 2013

Sometimes I think my life is part of a well written screenplay. I've probably noted that before but it holds true time after time. Today I went to see my stepfather for the first time in over twenty years. He lives about two hours away so came up here and met me at a local restaurant. I've only been to this place a few times but they have the best grilled cheese around and I like the decor.

He got there before me, and as I walked in and scanned the crowd I saw…Husband #2 and my ex-stepdaughter. Not who I expected. Though relations with him are nonexistent, and I was actually happy to see him and his daughter, it was odd timing. I swear my life is riddled with living symbols of the paths I've chosen. Somewhere up there a writer is thinking, "I know, I'll put her ex-husband in the scene and create a stepparent/stepchild parallel!"

I turned to my left and saw my stepfather. We hugged tightly and smiled and then I told him to hold on a second.

I ran back to the other table and told Husband #2 about the man I was meeting with. He said, "Really? Your stepdad?" He'd heard about him all the seven years we were together, but like me had assumed a reunion was out of the question. I nodded and replied. "Yes, it's been twenty years. Don't let that happen with Ivy." Then I turned to my ex-stepdaughter and gave her arm an affectionate squeeze.

I had a wonderful lunch with my stepfather. We had a lot to catch up on: where we've been the last bunch of years, who we've married and divorced. We've both had two of each in that time. I noticed that he chewed his cuticles. I nervously began to chew mine but caught myself. Guess I know where I got that trait from. He mentioned that he cooks all the time. Check. Me too. We talked about our jobs in the finance industry and our similarities. Seeing him as a human, and not a parent up on a pedestal, made any slip ups forgivable.

If I look back at my parenting skills, well, I've been far less than perfect. I did things I said I'd never do, exposed Ivy to situations that I was exposed to and hated. She will be the first to tell you that I've messed up. A lot. But at the core of it, I love her very much and would certainly have done things differently if I could have, if I had this wisdom back when I was young. But of course you don't get this wisdom without screwing up and making mistakes and hurting people and hurting yourself.

The important thing about making mistakes is learning from them, and not repeating them. Some people perpetually sabotage themselves and others and never figure it out. They go through life hating their exes and their parents, consumed always by blame and angst. We don't live forever and only get one chance here to do all we can to make peace for ourselves and others. We're not perfect but I think Dad and I have learned. We've got a ways to go. Only Jonathan Livingston Seagull and God have achieved perfection (and all the other deities out there). But we've learned. We'll make mistakes but hopefully not the same ones.

All the while at lunch I was looking over at Husband #2 and his daughter. Though he's been mostly out of our lives (entirely out in the last year) he "got" Ivy when she was four, the same age I got my Dad. Maybe I project my feelings of abandonment onto Ivy. Maybe she doesn't care that Husband #2 has moved on with his new wife and life and daughter. Maybe I need to let it go unless she brings it up. One of her teachers said I fight her battles for her, and that might be true. The ex and his daughter left without my noticing. I'll send him this blog and he can decide for himself what to do. I'd just hate for him to wait twenty years and then try to catch up to Ivy when it may be too late, and when now is the point in her life that everything really matters.

But back to MY table and MY life. There's no point rehashing all my dad and I talked about except that I have a sense of closure I didn't have a couple of weeks ago. The sad haunted feeling I've carried along for so much of my life seems to have vanished. You'd think something that heavy would be as hard to shed as my post-divorce weight. You would think it would take months of hard work to whittle down my neuroses. But it didn't.

Just seeing Dad for two hours over a grilled cheese sandwich and tomato soup helped that wounded little girl to grow up. I don't know what the future will bring but the present got a lot brighter.

To all the adult little girls out there, don't give up.

Running A Marathon

April 1, 2013

Lately I feel like I'm running a marathon. The end is in sight but damn far away. I'm exhausted and feel some days that I'm just not going to make it. I plod along, one day after another, after another. On a good day, a friendly face will be standing by the roadside with a glass of water. On bad days, I'm running alone. Ryan is on my cell phone in this analogy, chatting with me, urging me to soldier on, but I wish there were more people by the roadside, in real life, on my journey.

I've learned over the years, that as a single parent you can never stop running. I hear about people who get overwhelmed and take time out of work to travel or find themselves. I've never had that luxury. In both my marriages, I made more money. I was the one who paid the majority of the bills. The upside is that when I left, my income level didn't change much. But damn it would have been nice, or would be nice, to just stop running, for just a little while, and decompress.

Tonight, after a nice Easter dinner with family (a welcome respite that I enjoyed very much), I came home and just sat in the living room, staring off into space. It was a rough couple of weeks, and by the time I got home from a long drive it took all my energy to take Lily out then hunker down. Ivy went up to her room to study after a brief but painful argument. I sat on the recliner wrapped in a blanket. Henry and Lily (cat and dog) sat on my lap. I didn't want to watch TV or call anyone, or sleep, or listen to music. I just sat and stared across the room. It was the equivalent of staring at the ceiling but I was at the wrong angle for that.

I was thinking tonight that maybe I had reached my limit of what I can handle. None of it is major. No deaths, or cancer, or car repossession, or foreclosure. It's just too many little things I have to deal with on my own, all the while always looking strong for my daughter and happy to the outside world.

Tonight I just...stopped running. Maybe for an hour. Maybe longer. I don't know.

Last year Ivy was diagnosed with a potentially fatal genetic disorder. For now, she's fine except for chronic pain in her hands and feet that is somewhat controlled with medicine. But the last twelve months have been spent in doctor's offices with her being jabbed and scanned and tested, with me trying not to fall apart. Running and running and assuring her that things are fine, to keep her from falling apart. If this disease ever does fully kick in, it's treatable. With treatment it will never get worse and it will be fine—as fine as these things can get. She won't die. She'll be okay. And maybe it never will fully kick in. But it was about a year of not knowing that, of waiting for results. Ryan was there of course. At every doctor visit, every blood draw, he was there texting or calling. But it's hard going it alone, without a real hand to hold.

This is the year my second ex-husband chose to disappear from our lives. This is also the year my micro-family got even smaller. There was a death in family, which triggered some others to become even more distant than they were before. It was for the best but there was some venom that made everything harder and sadder.

Last month my check engine light went on. Not a big deal really but it took a month of taking it to the shop and trying different things to get it to go off for good. Several visits with my walking a half hour in each direction to and from the shop. I was overwhelmed and wished for the millionth time I had a husband—here—to help me with things. To pick me up and drop me off. Ryan and I are doing fine with this long distance arrangement, but don't underestimate the value of a real hug.

Two weeks ago, Ivy came home and told me that her friend ran over her feet. They looked all right but she could barely walk. It's a long story and all that matters for this blog is that my child was in pain, physical and emotional. I saw her, rattled and tired, crying, and it killed me. I could see too that she was done "running." The insurance claim has been filed now and the worst is behind us, but I really wished last week I had someone who could have made the calls for me. Could have let me sit this one out while I sat and stared at a wall to catch my breath.

Ivy is healing gradually and today started on a calm note but it changed. I was in the shower getting ready when Ivy ran upstairs to tell me there water was pouring out of the light fixture in the ceiling. I spent the day worrying about it. Was it a burst pipe? What was I supposed to do? Call a plumber? An insurance company? I didn't know, and once again I wished I could step out of the endless race and let someone else deal with things for me.

In the end, I talked to a friend on the phone and went to a neighbor's house who is a plumber (these are the type of folks who supply drinks in the marathon). Tuesday I'll learn how to caulk and I'll paint over the stain in the ceiling. New skills to help with my distance running.

The good things about being a single parent are that when things go well you get the credit, and there are no custody battles. You get the kid all the time. But the downside, you are the only one. It's all you and when you screw up, you are to blame. You are the disciplinarian, always the bad guy. Always the strong one, the shoulder, the cook, the cleaner, the bank.

And you can never stop running, even if your legs and mind are tired and you would do about anything for some sleep. I am grateful for the friends and family I have. And I am utterly relieved that once I'm in California I won't have to face things alone, as the only adult in what is supposed to be a two parent team. But I suspect this final stretch may very well be the hardest one yet.

Here's to a better month ahead.

Leaving Bedford Falls

April 14, 2013

In the movie *It's a Wonderful Life*, main character George Bailey spent his whole life trying to get out of Bedford Falls. He wanted to "see the world!" He planned and saved, packed his giant suitcase, but he never got to leave.

His life turned out all right in the end. He saw the impact he'd had on his small town, the lives he touched, how others' lives would have been if he'd never been born. I suppose we all have a little George Bailey in us. We have made a difference. No matter how much we may curse our lot in life, or think about our misfortune, we all know at the base of it, we're here because it's where we needed to be. If we'd chosen another path, everything would be different: all the events and people we love, and all the things that changed as a result of our presence without our ever even knowing it.

I liked the town I grew up in. It had its downsides like any town, but I mostly remember the small pond behind my house, and the Taunton Green, a grassy common that was our pride and joy. My first job was there, my first boyfriend, first heartbreak, first apartment, first pet (that was my own, not a family pet). It was the place where day by day I grew from a child to an adult. Like George, I spent a lot of time thinking about where I'd live someday. Over the years I moved to a few different towns but all within about twenty miles.

The first time I visited my real dad in western New York though, I thought about how beautiful it was. It was so lush and green. They talked differently than I did, had a different culture. They hunted and fished and went camping. Later he moved to an even more rural place that bordered an Amish village, and I was utterly enchanted. I was about nineteen then and longed to live somewhere that was foreign. But I stayed where I was. My sister moved from New York to Arizona and when I went to see her for the first time, I was floored by the beauty.

She had a lemon tree in her yard, or maybe a lime tree, not sure. The view from her front and backyard was mountains. The skies were clear and blue, and at night the stars were as bright as the ones I've had painted on my ceiling wherever I've lived. I wanted to move to Arizona. But I didn't. I stayed where I was.

When I left Ivy's father, when I was thirty, I went to Prince Edward Island for the first time. It was the most beautiful place I had ever seen. There were colors on the landscape more vibrant than any I'd seen in real life. The people were calm and friendly, the water warm, and mostly it was different from everything I knew. I wanted to move to PEI. I went so far as to go on a job interview. Not for just then, but to feel out the jobs there, for the next year. This was July and I'd decided that come that next April, I'd make the move. Ivy could go to kindergarten there the next fall and learn French, learn to step dance, maybe go to bagpipe school. I didn't go through with it. There was always something to tie me to New England. Then there was the temptation to move to Atlanta, settle there and try to transfer my job. The weather was warm and property inexpensive. And it was utterly different and new.

But I did not go there either. I stayed where I was. At some point I moved to the town I'm in now, where I've been eleven years. Just ninety miles from my home base. Same office, same job. Not much change at all except there were more hills here. I traded cranberry bogs for an endlessly lovely sparkling river. It's a wonderful small New England town. My own Bedford Falls.

I haven't been restless in a long time. Maybe it's age, or just acceptance that, like George Bailey, this is the only place I'd ever live. I stopped dreaming of faraway tropical places where I would start fresh, carve out a new life. Maybe it's because I was finally content with my Bedford Falls. I long ago stopped wishing everything was changed. Sure, I have had some hard days or years, but I get through.

But then when I least expected it, (as you all know from prior blog entries) everything changed, and now in about eighteen months I'll be starting anew, in a faraway land where nothing is familiar. Part of me is nervous and sad about leaving my Bedford Falls, but part feels like George Bailey when he was young, when he was about to board that train to his new and wonderful life. When he read *National Geographic* magazine and talked about all the distant lands he wanted to visit.

I have a feeling that if George had left Bedford Falls, wherever he would have landed, he would have touched lives and made a difference. He would have made friends and been successful and loved whatever exotic land he learned to call home.

George Bailey and I are not so different. I am going to embrace my new life in California with all its newness and adventure. It might be tough after forty-four years, but it's coming on time to leave Bedford Falls. George Bailey would be happy for me.

Feeling The Bombs In Boston

April 20, 2013

I was at work Monday afternoon in Boston, very focused on a spreadsheet. The mailroom guy ran up to me and said, "Did you hear what just happened?" I said no. He explained then there were just two explosions down the street at the Boston Marathon. Right then we all wondered if it was a gas leak or chemical explosion.

Except in the small bad sections of Boston, the rest is safe. It's a small quiet city and you can walk from one end to the other in about an hour or so. In the morning we heard a big BOOM. Someone asked, "What was that?" I said it sounded like a cannon. It was a cannon in fact, part of the Patriot's Day parade. Innocent. Traditional.

So when Joe mentioned the afternoon explosions I wondered if a decorative cannon misfired. By now the whole world knows what happened in Boston on Monday. Two brothers from Russia set bombs at the Boston Marathon. Three people died, many we injured and lost limbs. It was horrific and rattled us all.

I left work on Monday on the train before they limited travel, and worked from home the rest of the week. Our office closed Tuesday. The whole city was closed today. Literally, the entire city and surrounding towns shut down. People were forced to stay inside their homes, told not to answer their doors for anyone but police. "Do not open blinds or go outside." They coined a new term for it. "Shelter In." The subways, taxis, and commuter rail trains shut down. In my life I have never seen this. I don't think anyone has in the history of Boston. Everyday we've watched the TV as they first identified the bombers, killed the first one, and just hours ago shot and captured the second one. A policeman was killed too. More death on top of death.

I should be jumping up and down and cheering like everyone else. The bad guys are gone. We're safe! And I am relieved. I have missed Boston with its cobblestone and history. The North End and Haymarket and the Holocaust Memorial I pass each day on my walk from Boston Garden/Fleet Center/BankNorth Garden to my office.

But I'm too gripped with sadness to rejoice. I'm sad for the victims, the innocents who gathered around to cheer on the runners. I'm sad for the family and friends of them and for the families of the bad guys.

The bombers were young, twenty-six and nineteen. When I see the smiling face of the younger one I am disturbed. He has a sweet innocent look. How could this young boy who showed such promise have done this? Why? He was shot in a boat in Watertown, and then arrested. We are all waiting to hear what he has to say, why he did this.

But mostly, I look at him and see boys my daughter's age with their smiling faces and promise, their gregarious nature and kindness. It's not fair to compare the boys I know with him as this Russian boy DID commit unspeakable acts. He threw explosives out a window (or his brother did). He left bombs on a street and killed and maimed people. He will die in the hospital or prison, hopefully after he explains it all.

I'm not arguing his guilt. But I can't help but see his face, and wonder what happened. He was a young boy when he moved here, is an American by most standards. So why kill Americans? He is not a friend of my daughter, and her schoolmates are not like him. But it pains me that he was just an average likable kid until this happened.

I guess I'd feel better if he was a loner or imbalanced, or there were reams of paper about his unsteady mental state like the Colorado theater shooter, or clearly not right like the Sandy Hook shooter.

But this boy, Dzhokhar A. Tsarnaev . . . it's just sad.

I am pained by the actions of humans, of their disrespect for life, the ease with which life is over. The rapidity with which a day can go from normal to tragic, and your child can go from angel to devil to dead.

It puts everything in perspective, makes one appreciate life and freedom, makes one realize how little the little things matter.

I am glad the terror of this particular piece of history has ended but it was not without damage and harm both to victims, and to everyone who watched from their homes as just a little more innocence was lost. We all witnessed a slight erosion of humanity this week.

It's Friday night and I sincerely hope that the worst truly is over and we can all start to recover.

Visiting California

May 24, 2013

Last week I went to California to see Ryan. We hadn't seen each other since mid-February which was our longest stretch yet. And yes, time went by quickly, but those months in between were sometimes very difficult. It really is far better to hug someone than just email them. I had told him, jokingly, that once I arrived I was going to spend the whole short five day trip curled up on the couch, hugging him.

As it turned out, I was sick for most of the trip and did indeed curl up on the couch or in bed every chance I got. And despite my stomach hurting, and the nausea and the throbbing sinus headache that about five different over the counter meds didn't help, it was a nice visit. We were together and that's really all that mattered.

When I walked into the house after our nice ride through Topanga Canyon Road, he surprised me with flowers and a lovely card that said it was to celebrate the first "Carly is Amazing Day." We'd talked about flowers a few months ago. I mentioned that he'd never bought me flowers. He said, "You hate flowers." Incredulous, from my end of the phone, I replied. "What? No one hates flowers." He confessed then he'd gone out of his way to NOT buy me flowers because he thought I said in an early conversation that I didn't like getting them. So I was thrilled to get a big bouquet and a card with fuzzy puppies on it. What was just as nice though was that when I changed into my Happy

Bunny PJs and Great Gatsby t-shirt (sexy, I know) and switched from contacts to glasses, he was there to snuggle with me, get my ibuprofen, and was just so darn nice.

There's a lot to like about Ryan but his biggest attribute is that he's been consistently nice for about a year and a half. I know we don't see each other all that often but still, in all the long phone calls, one would expect a big fight at some point, a meltdown, a hissy fit. But no, he's just slow and steady and calm. A tortoise to my hare personality. He's a good egg. My good egg.

The next day was Ryan's big birthday party at his friends' house. It was wonderful. We picked up the cake and the entrée, and people brought food and drinks. His friends who hosted have known Ryan more than twenty years. It's the kind of party I always wanted to have for someone I loved, the kind you see in movies where friends come over and play music, and lights are strung outside in trees, and someone lights a fire pit, and the big crowd sings happy birthday, and the guy gets all shy because we're all giving him attention.

Sunday was my book signing. I've had signings before but not in CA, and not with these friends. Some were mine and some his, and now I guess we're all one group. What made the day more special was that Ryan was there too. He'd laid out the books, designed the covers, run them through his press. It was really fun having him there, interacting, mingling with friends. We make a good writing/publishing/life-in-general team.

Monday came and went. We drove through Ventura, just for fun. We stopped at a fruit stand and bought fresh cherries and strawberries. The thing about Southern California, even in their summer when most of the grass is yellow, is that everything is bright and sunny and pretty. It's as if Someone up above placed an enhancing filter over everything, and the emotions and colors and landscape…they all just POP. Could be because I'm in love of course. But I don't think it's just that. The skies are blue and clear, and they have this big yellow thing we don't see much back in Massachusetts. They call it SUN.

Before we knew it, Tuesday came and I had to get on a plane back to Boston. It was a bumpy seven hour flight and it was raining when I got back to the city. We had severe thunder and lightning storms all through the night and Lily never slept. Nor did I. The sun has been out since, but it's hiding itself under a thick cloud layer. I haven't seen a blue sky since Tuesday morning.

I'm going back to California in July with Ivy to look at colleges. I'm not sure if she will go to San Diego or Santa Barbara or stay back East. I'm certainly hoping she becomes enchanted with the west coast, as the idea of leaving her back here is too painful to even entertain. I'm constantly torn, wanting the next year to hurry and go by so we can move to California, but also wanting to slam on the brakes because Ivy is growing up so fast and in another year everything will change. Even if she comes to California, she'll live at school and her little girlhood will be in the past. For now, I'm just going on the assumption that we will move out as a family, pets in tow, and all live happily ever after.

There's nothing wrong with optimism.

Prelude To
An Empty Nest

June 18, 2013

A couple of years ago, Lily was born. Two months later, I bought her as part of my quest to swear off relationships forever, and bask in the unconditional love of a rebound dog. She's still a delight and I like that throughout the day when I'm home, she'll randomly look at me and wag her tail. I get frustrated with her sometimes but I love her. And clearly, she loves me.

Ryan loves me too and his texts and calls throughout the day are the human equivalent of a tail wag to remind me that he's around, and smitten. And I give him a virtual wag right back.

Ivy though, she's not as enamored of me as when she was four or five. She used to sit on my foot, or cling onto me like a Koala. It was heartwarming. But of course, kids grow up. We had a really good day last weekend though, shopping at the mall. It was the first day in a long time I can remember that we didn't have any conflict. It's not that we fight all the time, but as in any relationship, we have our days that we just can't seem to say the right thing to each other. I know it's half my fault. But that day it was just really nice, like old times.

We talked briefly about our upcoming trip to California to look at colleges for her. All pleasant. I told her she doesn't have to go away to college. She can live home and attend somewhere in L.A or in the next town and I didn't want her to think she HAD to live on campus. She interrupted calmly and said, "I don't want to move across the country. Why don't you get that?" I said, "I thought you'd softened on it." She said no, she just didn't want to get yelled at.

I couldn't help but think about a date I had many years ago. I'd dated someone a few months and then he broke up with me. We decided to try being friends, mostly because I didn't want to let go. We had a wonderful evening. Nice dinner, a movie. But then at some point I must have questioned why we broke up. I don't remember his words now but the jist of it was similar to Ivy's speech. He was having a great time and cared about me, he said, but my future and his weren't on the same path. I probably got about as silent then as I did with Ivy.

Ivy knew I was hurt. She said, "Don't be mad." I said I wasn't, just disappointed. And I hated saying that because it wasn't to make her feel guilty. I was just stunned and saddened. And like with that guy all those years ago, I can't blame her for wanting something different from me, even if at some point (most of her seventeen years) we've had the same path.

Who is to say where she will actually go to college? Maybe next month she will fall in love with the sun and sand and seals of San Diego, or the quaint downtown and boardwalk of Santa Barbara. Maybe the palm trees will entrance her. Maybe she'll see someone famous on the Santa Monica pier and become star struck. God I hope so. And if not, I guess it's time to accept that Ivy isn't four or five, and she's not Lily. Or Ryan. She's her own person.

The ground beneath my feet was unstable for most of my life and so I never felt inexorably settled in any one place. I strove to raise Ivy differently, to imbue her childhood town with a sense of home. That's a good thing, and healthy. But it might make it hard for her to ever live somewhere that's not here, in our little New England town.

I guess in the coming months we will all see how this unfolds. Where will she apply to school? Where will she get accepted? And where will she end up? Clinging to me like a Koala in CA or spreading her wings in a whole different part of the country?

Until then, I am readying for our trip out west to tour colleges. I don't know what the future will bring but I am savoring the present.

When The Bottom Falls Out

June 26, 2013

When I think of my childhood, one thing I remember fondly is my pen pal from England. We'll call her Polly. I connected with her through an agency listed in a magazine when we were both in fourth grade. I only remember bits and pieces of our correspondence but I loved getting her letters. They were in special airmail envelopes, thin as onion skin. I told her all about Garfield and she talked about Danger Mouse. We lost touch, I think around 6th grade.

After I had Ivy I wrote to her. Long story short, we missed each other in the mail and it took until a few years ago when she found me on Facebook that we finally began talking again. The reason this is all important is that she saved some of my letters. I hardly have anything left from when I was a kid so was thrilled to hear this. She sent the very first letter I wrote.

It was fun to read but I was surprised that it was from the autumn of 1977, when I was in fourth grade and still living in Rhode Island. It's funny that I misremembered it. I really thought we were in fifth grade, at a different point in my life. It's worth reading because I was so young and innocent. The cursive was sloppy but pretty. Very confident and happy.

Dear Polly,

I am nine years old. I got your name through International Pen Pals.
I live in a small town in Rhode Island with my Mother, Father, and brother
who is 13 years old. I have a dog named Buddy. He is a beagle.

I am in the fourth grade. I go to Cumberland Hill School. I am taking
skating lessons starting October 22. There is going to be a Halloween party at
my school October 30. I am going to be a Martian. How are you and what
grade are you in? Do you have any brothers and sisters or pets? Do you live in
the city or country? Please write soon. I am looking forward to hearing from
you. I am enclosing a picture of me. Your new friend, Carly.

When I read the letter, my heart sank because I knew that just
a few months later, the bottom fell out of my world. My stepfather
left us and we moved in the middle of the night to my grandparents'
house. I was awakened from a sound sleep and shuffled outside, leaving
many of my things behind. It was crowded at my grandparents' house.

My brother stayed in a section of their unfinished basement. He
rolled tinfoil floor to ceiling to make walls. He had strobe lights and
black light posters and played his music loud. His best friend he made
that year drowned in an icy pond. A couple of nights before the boy
died, his father showed up at our house asking where he was. The guy
was drunk and violent. I don't remember if we were hiding the boy or
not. When I think back on it, I just remember the man was scary and
looked like Albert Einstein and I was really proud of my grandfather
for standing up to him. I always wondered if the kid died on purpose
because he couldn't handle his dad anymore. I hope not.

My mom and I stayed in the living room. One of us on the couch,
one on a pull out cot. I don't remember now who slept where. Maybe
we switched off. I was in fourth grade, starting a new school as a pudgy
kid, whose world changed literally overnight. At the time though, I
rolled with the punches. My grandparents took me out for ice cream
a lot. And my aunt lived with us. She was really cool and very young
and went to the Disco every night (it seemed).

My mom and stepdad dated on weekends. She'd get all dressed up
and they'd go out. She lost weight and became glamorous again. She
was pretty before but she was dazzling when they went from married
to dating. Dad bought me lots of presents and brought my dog to visit

us sometimes. That year was the Blizzard of '78. My grandfather had a Jeep and we were one of the only families who could drive anywhere for supplies. Those days had a surreal feel to them. The things I remember… I got bunny and took him to Show and Tell and got my picture in the newspaper. I had a crush on a boy named George who looked like Luke Skywalker. But none of it felt real. I was detached from everything, watching it on a movie screen even then.

At the end of the school year, my parents got back together and we moved again. Another town, another school. I stayed in that place until I was an adult but nothing was ever the same. My biological dad wrote and wanted to see us after all those years. I've written about that before but what I didn't mention is that my brother quit school and moved away to New York for a while with that family. He was there, then gone suddenly. I was social enough on the outside, but spent a lot of time out in the woods with my beagle and a notebook. I stayed numb that whole time. Never really bounced back to the little girl I was when I wrote that first letter to Polly.

My brother came home at some point, and later my stepdad left again, for good. Well, until recently when he resurfaced and got in touch.

So when I got Polly's letters from that time, I was wistful reading that first one. A few days ago she sent another. The subject heading is January 1978. I haven't read it yet. I wanted to write part of this blog first, and then read the letter to see if there was anything in it that spoke of the turmoil we went through. Kids are resilient and can get through about anything. But it seems when we grow up, when we're out of survival mode, it hits us. And suddenly the rose-colored glasses we wore are torn from our faces, and we remember things differently, in the harsh bitter light of adulthood.

—Well, I just read it. It seems I lied to Polly. I wonder now if I lied because I was ashamed or because my mother told me not to tell anyone. The fact I lied tells me that I was numb and sad and shocked, just as I remembered. You can't see it in the letter, but knowing the real story, and comparing it to the sunny happy letter sent to Polly says it all. This letter lacks the confident cursive and is instead printed and sloppy.

Dear Polly,

I'm sorry I haven't written for so long but we moved. My father was transferred to Massachusetts. Now we live right near my grandmother. We were packing and moving all through the holidays. Thank you for my Christmas card it is so pretty.

I am going to a new school now, Richard's Avenue School. Mrs. Paull is my teacher. I am in the glee club. We practice one hour a week.

I take a bus to this school. I get on the bus in front of my house at 8:05am and I get home at 3:05. The schoolhouse is an old brick building...

Here's to mechanisms that help children cope, to tools we learn to put a positive spin on life events. And here's to Polly, who has brought back a slice of my childhood, well preserved on adorable stationary.

The Pursuit Of Happiness

August 1, 2013

When you're a parent, the pursuit of your own happiness is not what it's about. What life is comprised of is tallying up everything you wish your parents had done differently, and doing it right. Not that it happens mind you, but that's your goal. And you want your children to have everything you never did, be it stability, or a dad, or a house with a white picket fence, or freckles (yay, got one right). Mostly though, I have worked very hard and sacrificed so that Ivy can be happy, so that she will know peace.

I have structured my life, at least since she's been born, around what will make her life easier, and more solid. I spent more money than I should have to make that happen. I wanted good memories. I wanted trips to exotics places so that she wouldn't be afraid of travel or unfamiliar surroundings. When I left Husband #2, I stayed in this town even though it would have been much cheaper to move to New Hampshire. I remember seeing an ad for a little house on a lake. But I didn't want to pull her from her school system. And despite whatever else I've done wrong as a parent, I have always put her happiness and needs above mine. Except for that short stint when I dated that clown but, well, bygones. I had a slip. We all have slips.

So why is it that now, when Ivy is nearing "adulthood" and I am making preparations to sell our house, and mentally readying myself to relocate to California in a year, do I feel so guilty? Yes I suppose I could date Ryan long distance for another five years, so Ivy could attend a Massachusetts school at the low residential rate. But what then? I would sit home alone every night like I do now. There are only so many times I can watch *Mary and Max* or *Pitch Perfect*. Only so many pets I can manage to fill the void of not having someone's hand to hold. Staying in Massachusetts so Ivy can come home every couple of months and dash out to see her friends…maybe it is selfish but I would really rather move to California and marry Ryan.

This is our biggest hurdle as a mother daughter team. She does not want to move to California, and I do. Though it's not a daily fight, it has become our irreconcilable difference.

I feel like a bad mother, wrenching her from all she's known. But at the same time, once next August rolls around, no matter what happens, her life will be totally different. She'll live in a dorm room or apartment with strangers. Her comfort zone will be nonexistent. She will be hungry and have to feed herself, and wash her own clothes. And someone else will be complaining if her room is messy. She will have to walk or take a bus or long board to school. She will have to wake up when her alarm goes off.

And that will have nothing to do with where I'm living. It's college, the thing I have prepared her for since birth. The big stepping off point. The diving board into the unknown. And frankly, I would prefer she live an hour away from me if she hits the surface of the water and can't swim. Eventually she will learn to tread water, to go to her classes on time, to take her pills, and clean her clothes, and eat. But that first year especially, having her so far worries me.

And of course there is the fact that once I'm in California, she will by default, no longer be a Massachusetts resident and so we'll pay an arm and a leg (limbs I will need to sell to pay the tuition) for her to go to even a state school.

California does right by its residents. Even the really good schools are "affordable" if you make their state your home. There are worse things than waking up to a sunny sky and ocean waves each day.

And at the end of the day, even the move to California is for her happiness as much as mine. She doesn't see it yet, but moving will allow me to pay more of her tuition so it's not 100% financed. And she will have a stepfather. A good one this time who puts her feelings and needs first, who tries to understand her.

Moving to be with Ryan will give her a chance to see what a stepfather is supposed to be. She will see how men can be strong and loyal and fair and loving. She will witness her mother being treated with respect. She will be treated with respect. Eventually Ivy will accept that sometimes you have to make sacrifices for the people you love, and will understand that I am pursuing happiness for all of us. Not just for me.

Adopted Families

September 12, 2013

Growing up I had a very small nuclear family. As the years passed and people left or died or drifted off, it grew even smaller. I have a brother but we haven't spoken in many, many years and were never close. I have a sister on my dad's side but I've only seen her a handful of times. In short, I never got to experience big family parties as a child. We didn't have crowded Christmases or reunions. It was a fine enough way to grow up but I guess kids from smaller families always wonder how the other half lives.

When I met Ivy's dad, when I was twenty-one and had been on my own three years, I was entranced by his family. He is the oldest of four children. I spent ten years with Ivy's dad, and even though the marriage had to dissolve for a number of reasons, and we very rarely see him, I grabbed onto that family and never let go. My in-laws are still my in-laws even though I married and divorced someone else since then. That was almost a quarter of a century ago but when I think of family I think of them.

Though I've dated other people over the years, and most of their parents were terribly nice and welcoming, I've never gotten that same sense of permanence and warmth as I did that first time I went to meet Mr. and Mrs G. back in 1990.

Until now. About a week and half ago, Ryan flew me to Minnesota to meet his parents. I was excited to meet them, to learn more about Ryan. Till then I'd only met his little brother and his family in CA. Though that brother flew in for this impromptu family reunion, his sister from Indiana and her husband were there as well. Ryan's older brother and family live within walking distance to the parents' house in Minnesota so he was there as well as his children and some grandchildren. So many people, all in one spot, all family.

There was something familiar and warm about the house though, even before I walked in and met anyone. I have posted before, ad nauseam, about the sense of home I've really ever only felt at my grandparent's house. I've had glimpses of it in other places but their house was always my haven and escape from anything or anyone I needed to run from. When I walked into Ryan's parents' house, with its paneled walls and hutch cabinets, collection of horror films and *Twilight Zone* memorabilia, I recalled many childhood memories of my grandparents' place and hence became filled with a happy familiarity.

I was only there for a long weekend, as my vacation days are running out , but it was a very nice few days. I am reluctant to say fun. It was more than amusing. It was touching. One day Ryan and I took a road trip to a town where he had lived briefly as a child. Watching his eyes light up when he found his old house was truly wonderful. He circled the block round and round to see the house from different angles, to point out where he used to play, where the grocery store used to be. And what was even more touching was when he went back to his folks and showed his whole family the phone pictures. They laughed and reminisced together, and it was wonderful to watch.

His sister had created a photo album for his mother with family pictures from early childhood to recent times. I was stunned and thrilled to see a couple of me in there. Well, Ryan and me. She had scoured our Facebook posts to find pictures of us together so I would feel welcome, and I guess because she wanted the whole family captured in the book.

I wasn't treated like a guest but like someone who belonged there. No pretense, no airs to put on. I simply squished into the corner of the couch with Ryan and held his hand, engaged with his family, and smiled as I thought about my future life.

If I have learned nothing else from all my failures and successes in life so far, it's that families extend far beyond the biological ones we're born into. At any time, someone can walk into your life (or onto your Facebook page as the case may be) and adopt you. And before you know it, you have a whole new family to welcome you with open arms. And don't worry, I'm keeping the other ones of course, but you can never have too much love.

Good night all.

The Last September

September 26, 2013

The leaves are still green, the grass continues to grow lush and thick, and until three days ago I still needed the air conditioning in the house. But September is nearly over, and as it passes I can't help but think of this as one of the most stark realities of my future cross country move. People always talk about spring as being the season of rebirth, or of June marking the summer with its freedom and sunshine and possibilities.

But to me, September is the month of beginnings. It's been a painfully long time since I was in my K-12 years but September was always the time of fresh starts. Nothing marked life for a New England child like the first month of school. It was the month you put away your shorts and t-shirts, dragged out your corduroys and heavy sweaters. You bought new penny loafers and pencils, notebooks, and a new box of Crayola crayons, and life began anew. You knew you were facing nine months of studying and socializing with friends, and come June, it would be over. That year of your life would end, for better or worse, never to be repeated.

September is when you shift from stifling summer heat and mosquito bites, to cool air, seeing your breath, and to leaves crunching under your feet. The landscape changes from green to fire colored. September is a dropping off point when you gear up for the next adventure in your life. Instead of school, this last September in New England is the beginning of my next big step.

Ivy started her senior year in high school and will be applying to colleges soon. I have been clearing our house of all the accumulations that don't matter. I've tweaked my financial spreadsheet to project into next year. I invited a realtor in to talk about selling my house come spring. She spent a few hours at my place, going over what I needed to paint or fix. All minor stuff. And through her whole visit, what floored me, was that I was kind of excited. Relieved, not scared, not possessing my usual panic whenever a relationship inches ahead. Just excited that I was working on being a little closer to the new life.

I can't stress enough how out of character that is for me. I don't think I've ever had a relationship that wasn't fraught with anxiety and doubt. Even the really good relationships I've had (which is relative because they didn't stay good long) were plagued with my continual racing thoughts about all the reasons I shouldn't be there.

Yet here I am, with my new loafers and notebooks, facing nine months of packing and painting and getting ready, and socializing with friends. And come June, it's over. And though a big part of me is sad that the life I've had just with Ivy will also be over, I think it's time we let someone new into our life.

I imagine each month before the move new revelations will come up but this special month, this is the turning point.

Has it Really Been Two Years?

October 23, 2013

The other day, Ivy told me it was her sixth month anniversary with her boyfriend. I replied, "It's been two years for Ryan and me." She looked at me funny and said, "Two years from what? It's not even a real thing." She was somewhat joking but I could see her point. How exactly do you measure an online long distance relationship?

With tangible local relationships, the marker is the first time you meet someone at a party, or in an auto parts store (Ivy's dad). Other times it's the first real date, or the first time you sleep with someone if there's been some ambivalence before then. With us, it was marked by the first time I heard his voice. It was our first call after months of emails and texts and Facebook messages.

That particular night stood out for several reasons. Husband #2 was getting married the next day so a friend took me out (long story, she was his ex before me) and we got drinks. Strong drinks as I recall. I had two and had trouble walking to the car. No, I didn't drive. Ryan had called me right before our dinner and so I was a little giddy even before the Appletinis. "I really like this guy from California," I kept saying. Later that night when he called me back, I told him so.

"I really like you," I said. Until then we had danced around the concept of a relationship, hadn't said more than how nice it was to share emails. I don't know if either of us can say for sure when we "knew" only that October 21st two years ago we said it out loud.

My mother said recently that it's just hitting her I'm leaving. She assumed something would happen before now, no doubt my commitment issue would kick in, or I'd discover Ryan was a fraud or mean. But here we are. It's a real thing.

I went to California a few weeks ago and as part of my visit with Ryan, we went to Santa Barbara for a third time to see the college campus I'd love Ivy to attend. Thus far, she's still on the fence, meaning she doesn't really want to go but hasn't come up with a good alternative to stay in Massachusetts. I've assumed if I tread lightly she will follow along to the other coast and grow to love the sunny days and palm trees, the streets on grids and dry warm air, the mountains and blue skies. Yesterday though she brought home a brochure from a school up in New Hampshire. A pretty and very small school nestled in the mountains. I viewed their website and coincidentally it looks just like the college campus we live on now, half of which was sold to a developer who built condos on it. I wonder if she's even made the connection. I can see why it makes her feel like home.

I would love to discourage her from it, to have a reason to say it's not for her, which has been so easy with other colleges that are truly not right for her, but alas, this one is enticing. We are going to see it in November. I told her today I'd hoped she would love Santa Barbara as much as I did but it's fine that she doesn't. She's not me. Ivy says I always hated hot weather and I've changed. I haven't though. I'm just tired of darkness and gray skies and all the past bleakness both literal and figurative. There is a lot of good here, and people I will miss, but there is something about sunshine that draws me in, pulls me to the other side. Maybe it's the newness or the brightness. I'm not the first person to run out west in search of dream fulfillment.

The leaves outside are orange and yellow and red, the air is cooling. Hood shipped five varieties of eggnog to our grocery store. Autumn is here and with it the beginning of college applications and life plans. It's a time of decisions and acceptance and life changes.

The last two years went by very quickly. The fall will pass as fast, then winter, then spring, and before we know it summer will arrive. I don't know what the next months will bring but I am happy with Ryan and look forward to more of this real thing we have going.

Treading Water

December 10, 2013

Ivy and I had a wonderful Thanksgiving. We spent it with Ivy's Dad's family. Ivy's Dad wasn't there. He is absent from nearly all aspects of our lives. I haven't discussed him much, out of privacy, and won't now except to say that in many ways, he's in over his head. When we first split up, he slid from a regular life, to another more dangerous and sad one. We look at him and think, "How can he live like that?"

I mention this because we all have limits of what we can and do live with or without. And sometimes things get so out of hand, we don't realize how far it's gone or how bad it is. And that's how we live in situations others say they couldn't tolerate.

When I was with Husband #2, the control freak who "kept me on a diet" for seven years, I'd panic if I gained two or three pounds. Then after we split, I gained another two and another two. I see how tubby I am, and wonder how this got out of control. But I manage. I bought bigger clothes. If I saw Husband #2 on the street, he would look at me and wonder how I could be happy living in my own pudgy skin. I'm happy enough. It's not as out of control as he would think. It's a matter of perspective.

I've got a lot of credit card debt too. Just like the weight gain, it snuck up on me a bit at a time. I juggle it. It's a nonstop juggling act but I pay everything on time, usually extra. I'm treading water until I can sell my place and move to California, where I'll be sharing my expenses with Ryan. Some people, like Ryan, look at my mountain of debt and are speechless. They wonder how I can live like that, with so much owed.

A few years ago, one of the local moms said, "I don't know how you do it. I could never be a single mom." I'm not sure if that was a slight or she respected me for it. I told her that if she was forced into the situation, she'd figure it out. I find that when we tread water long enough, we find ourselves comfortable in that pond, and that becomes the new normal. We forget we're treading water. We call it living.

Humans only feel comfortable with what they know, what they've experienced. They point fingers at others, astonished they could live with fat or poverty or abuse, or live in a tiny apartment or a condo or a mansion. Or hell, a house full of cats.

On the way home from Thanksgiving dinner, I blew a tire. I ended up having to get four new ones. It cost an unexpected $650. Credit card debt. Today I took my car in for an oil change and was told I also needed spark plugs. Long story short, I paid almost $500 for various things. The clincher is, the mechanic said I need something else done that will cost $1500. I panicked. Where the hell was I going to get another $1500?

I came home and took a nap. When I awoke, I had calmed down. The car repair is just more credit card debt, more money owed, more water to tread. It's not cancer, or death, or job loss. I'm not being evicted. And I don't shop in the Big Girl section of the clothing store yet.

I think of Ivy's dad and how he lives. He seems okay with the road he chose. He has grown comfortable. No matter how much we wish he lived differently, he's not going to. Maybe forty-five is the age where all of a sudden everything clicks in. When we realize there's no point being upset over what we can't change, and that eventually, one way or the other, things work out. Maybe not the way we want, but somehow, things settle down.

I'm hoping when I start the next chapter of my life, I am able to reduce debt and reduce my weight. Until then though, I'm doing all right even if some people worry that I'm not like them. I resist the temptation to tell others they should live a certain way. Life is what it is.

Here's to treading water.

A Visit From
A Ghost In My Past

January 14, 2014

I was cleaning out some drawers last week and found two letters that upset me so much, it's taken me a week to write about them. One was a handwritten list entitled, "Things to never forget." I must have written it shortly after leaving Husband #2, almost seven years ago.

The list was comprised of all the terrible things he ever did to me, or as many as I could fit on two sides of lined paper. Looking back, there were lots more. Seven years of injustices and meanness. I clearly wrote it so I wouldn't ever be tempted to go back to him, to "fall for his niceness" which is what Ivy as a child used to say. It was bad stuff. He didn't beat me or cheat, but he did a lot of emotional stuff I never, ever should have put up with. I'm so much stronger now that sometimes I forgot how fragile I was then, how willing I was to put up with anything for the promise of love. I say the "promise of" because it was perpetually out of my reach for the whole relationship. He'd convinced me that if certain conditions were met, then he'd really love me and be happy. It never happened.

Needless to say, I became very sad upon reading it. I didn't want to remember I was ever that way. Who would?

I have a friend I've known forever. At one point in our lives I saw her after a long absence. We were both thin. This was between husband #1 and #2. She told me in the years we hadn't seen each other she'd gotten really heavy but then lost the weight. She showed me a "before" picture and I was both shocked and proud of her. One night I was at her place and someone was showing a video from her heavy time period. She came into view on the screen. I'd seen the picture so wasn't surprised, but when she saw herself, she ran from the room crying and screamed for us to shut it off. That's how I felt when I saw that letter to me.

The worse part was the other handwritten letter. It was a random notebook page recording a day from a trip Ivy and I took to New Orleans when she was only six or seven. I wrote about a cemetery tour and a night ghost tour. I also wrote how sad I was that when I called Husband #2 he told me he was going to be really busy when I got back and he didn't want to hear me complaining about it. I wrote that I'd hoped he say he missed me, but as usual, he was just pushing me away. There was more, but that's enough to paint a picture of a young woman who had such low self-esteem that she wrote about her acceptance of being treated that way, and giving up. The bigger issue is that we weren't even living together yet. Not engaged, not married. I could and SHOULD have easily walked away. But I stayed another four years. And married him for God's sake.

I hate that other me. I want to go back and kick the crap out her, to shake her and tell her how much unnecessary pain she's about to inflict on herself and her little girl. The notes made me hate him all over again. It was an emotional afternoon.

It's just another reason that the big move to California will be good for me. It will put distance between me and the past that lurks around every corner. They say, "Wherever you're going, there you are." But sometimes you can leave the weak sick person you were buried in the basement under concrete, and never look back. That's what I'm banking on.

Letting Go Of Living Alone

February 24, 2014

Last week I watched several episodes of *Murder She Wrote* on Netflix. It's been years since I've seen the show. Watching Jessica content on her own made me smile. For a moment I pictured myself at that age, writing books, walking along the beach alone. Then I remembered that even though I've been living alone (without a guy) for a few years, I'm not single. There's Ryan, waiting in the distance. And when I'm Jessica Fletcher's age, I'll be writing books with him by my side, or walking along the beach with me.

Even though in reality I will be moving to California in August, part of me is stuck in the rut of seeing myself as alone. Last week the realtor came over and took pictures of my house. I opened bank accounts in California. Ivy registered for school in Santa Barbara. In short, I'm on a near path to being a California resident. With Ryan. And yet I don't think it will hit me that I'm "in a relationship" until I'm out there. And even then, the concept of permanence will take a while to sink in.

Sometimes I feel like the mother in Chocolat, moving with the wind, gathering her daughter into her read cloak and starting over. Because really, except for the red cloak, that's been my life. Grabbing my daughter and starting life with her over and over again, and eating chocolate.

Last night I walked into Ivy's room. It's very clean, and staged for potential buyers. It's what the realtor called, "A dream bedroom."

She's got walls in several pastel colors, light strings on the walls, puppy posters and pictures of childhood times. Stuffed animals and little girl items fill the room. It struck me that when we move into the new place, she won't have a little girl room anymore. We're not getting rid of her things, but I imagine it will have a more grown up look to it. Her main home will be her college apartment and I will be the equivalent of a weekend parent for the first time in my life. I'll be getting holidays and school breaks, weekends when she wants.

I've been hoping desperately that we will sell the place quickly, and stay in a temporary apartment until we drive to California with the pets on a road trip, and start our next chapter. But last night…Seeing her room, and reflecting on Jessica Fletcher, drove home the end of this era. As Ryan would say, it is the natural progression of things. It isn't easy though. Regardless of the move, it's time for the next stage.

I'm enthusiastic about moving, about leaving, about not living a mile from an ex-husband who doesn't speak to us, about being nice and warm every day, about officially starting our future. About no longer having to do all the grown up stuff alone. I'm excited to have a best friend I get to live with.

But there will always be a part of me that thinks wistfully of Ivy's pink bedroom and miss the time when she was a little girl and it was just going to be us forever. When I first started corresponding with Ryan, back before we knew we had something between us, I had told him that I was content to be alone, had no interest in a relationship ever again. I'd told him my therapist said it was time for "a new dream," to scrap the one about the big house in the suburbs, with the SUV, and a husband. He argued that was stupid advice and giving up on love this young wasn't being fair to myself. I'm paraphrasing. That was the old dream, the goal, but growing old alone with a kid was the reality I'd accepted, maybe always expected.

So I'm giving up the dream of a big house in the suburbs (because it's a lot to clean and SoCal is prohibitively expensive). And on the SUV because we don't need one now. But I'm also relinquishing the lingering image of living alone in a little cottage with a dog. I am however keeping the image of the cottage and the dog. I'm adding in Ryan. Here's to accepting the new dreams.

Used Cars And Used Men: A Buyer's Guide To Dating

April 5, 2014

A friend of mine just finalized her divorce and has entered the murky waters of online dating. After ten years in her marriage, she is hungry for a new relationship with its promise of fulfillment and happiness, tenderness, honesty, intimacy. In short, a promise to deliver all that her marriage, by the end if it, did not. Anyone who has been divorced or ended a long-term relationship can relate. First there is the grieving period, then the anger, then the prospect of facing the dismal reality of what you really left. And finally, there is hope. Dating sites and hungry men capitalize on that hope.

It's been a few years since I've been on one of those sites, being happily nestled with my Ryan, and counting the days until I'm westward bound to start our life together. Watching her on the sites though, and hearing feedback, reminds me of where I was fifteen years ago, after my first divorce, and again after my second.

What I am seeing from her, and what mirrors exactly what I experienced, is a giddiness about how many men are out there. "Like shooting fish in a barrel," I told her the other day. Each one of them with a story, a well-rehearsed and usually well-written advertisement of all they have to offer, and a plea to the potential matches, "Please contact me if you're my forever love."

Blech! That's what I say about that. I was thinking last night that the difference between the Carly now, and the Carly many years ago, is that I can see flaws better. Age and experience are great teachers. It used to be, I would look at the ads, find someone attractive, read his profile, and depending on the pics and certain key terms: plays guitar, writer, creative, I would gloss over the unsavory aspects. Things like: heavy drinker, married five times, hates kids, hates dogs, not looking for long-term relationship...

Because surely, once I made a connection with this guy, all those traits would somehow disappear. He'd WANT commitment after he met me. He'd become responsible, quit smoking, etc. Of course it doesn't work that way. I should have learned that from my failed relationships. But there's something enticing about shopping for a future husband the way you shop for a used car.

I compare the experience to the difference between a sixteen year old boy and a fifty year old man each walking onto a used car lot with five thousand dollars in his pocket.

The sixteen year old boy will walk onto the lot planning to leave with a car that same day. Any car. Because that lot contains all the cars in the world and he'd better pick one. He'll look past the square gray cars, instead focusing on a red-hot two-seater with a convertible top. He won't read the specs on the car, about how many owners it's had, or how many accidents. The broken frame from one too many breakups/ crashes will not be evident. Several months later, the problems with the sexy car will surface. It will become high maintenance. There won't be new problems, only ones he pretended weren't there at the onset. He'll return to the lot, trade the car in. And he will start again. Based on my experience, you have to "buy a lot of used cars" before you learn to kick the tires and ask about history. At some point, you realize that the stuff that matters isn't on the surface. A fancy paint job does not correlate to being a good husband.

The fifty-year-old man will walk onto that same lot. He'll look under the hood, look for important things like one long-term owner, four doors, good gas mileage. Minor accidents acceptable but broken and repaired frames will inevitably break again. The man will check the cars over thoroughly. Not that his eyes won't light up at that red-hot two door convertible, but he's had enough of those to know that over time, the thrill wears off. And that man may very well return to the lot several times before he buys any of those cars, because he knows there are tons of single people and scads of used cars on any given day.

I am glad to be done shopping, but it is fun to watch my friend, sharing with her the hope of things to come.

Owl's Nests And Moving On

June 4, 2014

I haven't written a Carly blog in a long time. Life has been busy. Ivy graduates from high school on Friday. In a week, Ivy and I will take our cat to California to live with Ryan. And two weeks later, we will leave the home we've lived in for seven years to stay with friends for a month until the big move August 1st.

In the course of the last week, my home has gone from being clean and lovely, cozy and filled with items I've used to make my house a home, to rooms with bare bookshelves and cardboard boxes littering the floor. All the traces of Carly are being stripped off and stored, bringing the place mostly back to the plain cold townhouse it was when I bought it.

About a week ago I was outside within about thirty feet of my front door, when I glanced up at the rotted tree by the main street. It's a hollowed out tree riddled with woodpecker holes. An owl sat perched in a black hole by the top of the tree. I did a double take then accepted it really was a big old owl, sound asleep. I took pictures until he saw me and darted deep into the tree to hide. After that, I made a habit of checking on him each morning, a happy ritual. A few nights ago, Ivy and I went out and listened to him as he gurgled and fluttered and who-who-whoed in the darkness. It was peaceful and comforting.

Two days ago I came home and saw that the condo landscapers

had cut the tree down while I was working. I rounded the corner and found hunks of tree lying on the ground, the owl's former hiding place ravaged and tossed carelessly about. I was heartbroken. I'd really come to enjoy my daily sightings. I knelt on the ground and searched for a nest and eggs, pulling the innards from the hollowed tree. I saw only the owl's abode, an empty nest that he had made cozy for one. Twigs and leaves and fluff filled the inside of the tree. He had worked very hard to make his house a home. Poor sad little owl.

That evening I went out to walk Lily and heard the now familiar gurgle. I was surprised and happy so followed the sound until I came upon him sitting in one of the new short skinny trees. He was a fat owl on a small thin branch, a temporary home. He would someday find a new place to live, I knew, but until then he sat up there, just above his old place, close but not on his old homestead.

I went back in the house and considered the parallel. I have made this my current home for the last seven years. I have filled it with the human equivalent of twigs and leaves and fluff. My condo, knock on wood, was not decimated before my eyes, but soon I will be leaving it. And when I look back, I will see all my homey things removed. I will check the bedrooms for eggs, or baby owls, but my little human owl will be gone.

And I will move just down the street in a place that is good for temporary living, a fat little owl on a thin branch. I will sometimes walk by this old house and look at it from afar and recall that it is a place I used to live in with my daughter. And eventually, in my case August 1st, we will get in our car with my rebound dog Lily and head to what I hope is our forever home. And once again I will gather twigs and leaves and fluff and make the new place my home.

Some people love to visit their old houses, places where they grew up, or got married or divorced. Places they had their first kiss, or bought their first car. I'm not in that school. I don't like going back to the old tree, thinking about how things were or weren't. It depresses me. I've done it, to see if the reality is the same as memory, but I don't particularly like it.

I saw and heard the owl again last night, in the new skinny tree. He needs time to mentally adjust, to plan, to mourn his home before he

flies off to a whole new life and unfamiliar surroundings. I can relate.
I think my temporary apartment, within walking distance of this one,
is just what I need to wean myself before I move off to a whole new
life and unfamiliar surroundings.

I will miss my owl, and I will miss the house with all the memories
and Carly/Ivy life events it held. But soon I too will fly off and begin
work on a new nest with my baby owl daughter and my rebound dog.

Happy nesting.

Leaving Bradfield

July 20, 2014

Ivy and I moved out of our home three weeks ago. We stripped every trace of us from the place. Since then, we have been staying with friends A week from now, Ivy, Lily, and I will hop in my Mini Cooper and start our 3,000 mile drive to Simi Valley, to Ryan, and to our new life. All the tasks have been completed: utilities set up at the new place, addresses and bank accounts changed, car checked by mechanic, dog groomed, Ryan's house packed and ready, appliances purchased, goodbyes said (some of them). There were a million little details to tend to but they are complete.

I told Ivy the other day that in many ways it's like I'm going away to college too. Back in 1986 I was supposed to go. Mom escorted me to the college in the late spring for orientation. I was excited for this brand-new life. It was meant to be the time I moved away, grew up a little, cut the apron strings. I didn't go away to college after all. I moved out a few months later so did grow up, abruptly, but I never made the jump to a new life per se. I've always lived within ninety miles of where I was born. Sure I've been married and divorced, twice, and had relationships and a child, and jobs. But I've never made a big change.

This will be different for all of us, but like in the 1980's I am excited about the potential for a new life. About the adventure and newness. I will miss the people here, and the old, historical life that flows through New England: the aged homes and ivy covered brick walls, and the cobblestone streets of Boston. I'll miss my town, and my prior towns, and certainly Boston, where I've spent the last twenty-five years working.

But there comes a time when I need to step out of the warm hug that is Bradfield and experience the rest of the country, where people pronounce Rs and have healthy vitamin D levels in their blood, and go to movies on sunny Saturdays without panicking it will be the last one for months. Where every night is sit out on the patio and grill out night, and you can go outdoors and eat ice cream in February in your shorts and sandals. I want to learn different highways and town names, check books out of new libraries. And of course at the base of it, I want to be with Ryan and start our life together. That's what it's really all about when you get down to it. The adventure would not be fun or doable, if not for him.

If he hadn't come around, posted on my Facebook page that particular day, I probably would have stayed here forever and been content, and been one of those people who rolls her eyes when someone mentions Southern California. "Earthquakes and wildfires," I'd say. "You couldn't pay me enough to live there." But he pointed out things about California I didn't know. Taught me things about love I didn't know. He gave me new perspective.

I don't mind being a hypocrite. There's nothing wrong with changing your mind when you have new information. In my early Carly blogs I stated I'd never date again, that relationships were impossible for me. I was bitter and didn't know that love was in the cards for me after all. And I didn't know that California has plenty of charm too. Different maybe, but it's there.

This will be my last blog from Bradfield. The next one may be from the road or when I'm settled in our new home. It will not be easy to leave but it would be harder to stay, knowing all that's out there.

Leaving Bradfield will be a sad day indeed, but it provided the most important twelve-year backdrop of my life. I've done more growing up and changing here than in all my other years.

I will miss you, New England.

Home At Last

September 2, 2014

It's been too long since I've written a blog. So much has changed since the last post and I wonder how to cram it all into one entry. I'll do my best.

I'll first say that I don't recall a time when I've ever felt this much at peace and so content in my life. There have been moments of extreme happiness of course, but they were always peppered with angst or regret or drama. There was always the threat of doom around the corner. Sometimes it was just in my head, a knee-jerk reaction to rugs being pulled out from under me over the years. But often, there really was a gray cloud hanging above.

With Ryan, I've always had a sense of peace. From the first few conversations we had, I knew this relationship was different. My normal sense of self-doubt was lacking. My typical get-close-then-panic and run reflex was blessedly absent. With all that happened in those three years of waiting to relocate: Ivy's diagnosis, some painful family conflict, selling my townhouse, watching as one ex continued to spiral out of control with drugs and alcohol, while another remarried, stopped speaking to Ivy and me, and then had a baby with the new wife, the pleasant reemergence of my stepfather after twenty years... Amidst all of that, I never got cold feet about my decision to move to California with Ryan.

The cross-country drive with Ivy and Lily (my rebound dog) was wonderful. We had four days of rain, but we're used to rain. Ivy and I listened to audio books, and streamed comedy shows. We laughed a lot, and sang along to iTunes, and ate out at drive-through places almost every meal. We took a quick side trip to Niagara Falls. It was nice, this last big mother-daughter trip before I moved in with Ryan, and Ivy went off to college to grow up and change forever.

The first week we arrived in California was tough. There was a heat wave, and we had no air conditioning. Ivy got stuck with the smallest room in the bungalow she was renting, and her bunkmate was "weird." She came home a lot the first month and it pained me that moving out here was so hard for her. That it was my fault. That I'd displaced her and caused her sadness.

Ryan got a call that his mother back in Minnesota was ill and probably not going to make it much longer. And did I mention how HOT it was. There were days we sat on the couch as sweat poured down our faces. And the flies...so many flies because there weren't screens on all the windows.

But even with that, it was still really nice to be here. It was peaceful, and I marveled at the landscape and the lizards, the palm trees and sunsets. The first time I drove to the office at five in the morning and saw the lighted cross on Rocky Peak, it took my breath away. I felt something long forgotten. Faith. Maybe not in God per se but a belief that things were going along exactly as planned.

I see beauty every day in the hills and mountains, in my hummingbird feeder, in the dragon flies, in the arroyo next door with its egrets and ducks. I smile at the coziness of the house, how Ryan's and my things complement each other and make this old ranch house a home.

The heat wave broke, new screens were installed. Ivy became accustomed to her new life, and her roommate moved out and was replaced with someone "very nice." I like to think Ivy too marvels at the beauty of the ocean and the mountains and palm trees by her school. She calls me sometimes (not every day) and tells me about trips to the grocery store, or something she's cooked all by herself, or a new restaurant she's discovered. The fact she doesn't need me as much tells me she's also okay with this path, and maybe for her too everything is going as it should.

Ryan's mother passed away a couple of weeks ago. He is visiting his father in Minnesota this week. I didn't know how I'd be, here alone in this new house, in this strange town. But as I told him last night, I feel like we've always lived here. It felt like home when I walked through the door, and it's hard to remember a life, just a short time ago, when I wasn't here.

The sun shines, and a heavy cool breeze blows through the house, whipping the curtains about and reviving me, bringing me to life. Wrapping me in a warmth and happiness I had only dreamt of.

Good night from California.

Goodbye 2015

December 31, 2015

I haven't written a blog in a long time. Maybe I've been too busy, or too content. But here it is, New Year's Eve 2015 and too much time has passed.

I'll start by saying that even with some ups and downs this year, it's been the most peaceful year that I can remember. Work has been stressful but about halfway through the year I had a paradigm shift in my thinking. It's just a job. Only a job. I'm not a surgeon or a teacher or a politician. I work for a bank. Enabling myself to realize that though my function is important to the process, it's not life changing and not worthy of any emotional angst I awarded it.

My company works with a charity called Spark that brings eighth grade children to the office once a week in ten week shifts. We are matched one on one and mentor the students to take what interests them and show them how to make a career out of it. I did two shifts, one in March and another in August. The first little girl was an artist and the second a budding novelist. Both experiences were wonderful and rewarding. I will be working with the second girl this March when we will learn about screenwriting. I feel fortunate to be working with such great kids and am thankful for the charity that brought us together.

Ryan and I are fine. We are comfortable and have very little conflict. I think the combination of being older, more passive, and compatible is key. I told Ivy recently that Ryan tolerates me better than anyone I've ever met. I suppose if there is a downside, it's that we are so content with each other, watching old movies and hanging around in our cozy house, that we border on being antisocial. I don't think that is a bad thing but we should maybe venture out more in 2016. For the first time in my life, I am placid most of the time. Things are easy and peaceful and I no longer worry about a shoe dropping. It's just...nice.

Ivy is in her second year of college, starting her fourth semester. She's endured her share of drama at school but that is part of the growing up process. I have worked very hard not to micromanage and fix. This has been my biggest challenge. But she met a nice boy the beginning of the year and, as with Ryan and me, I think he helps to balance her.

After months of not writing a single word of fiction, all of a sudden I am back on track. I've written a bunch of new stories, sold a few, wrote a novel, and a screenplay. I am back to my productive too-much-coffee, too-little-sleep self but without the inner angst.

And finally, I lost the weight I've lamented about for years. I still have a bit to go but I'm getting there. Looking forward to whatever 2016 brings.

Happy New Year to all!

The Benefits Of Poverty

January 14, 2016

When I was small, we didn't have much money. Back then, people didn't live off credit cards. If you couldn't afford something you saved until you could have it. We didn't buy impulse things. We made lists for Santa, and for parents at birthday time. We got new school clothes once a year and those were put on layaway for several weeks. When early September came and we went to K-Mart or Bradlees to pick up the box of layaway treasures it was always one of the most exciting days of the year.

I could probably name every time we ever went out to a fancy dinner. It was rare and special. When we went grocery shopping, we had a list. We didn't buy everything on the shelf that looked yummy; we got what we needed and made it last, usually long enough until the next payday.

For entertainment we played games or went out to play or watched television. I spent a lot of time with my beagle, and my notebook in which I wrote stories. We went to the flea market and browsed. We visited family. When I was in high school I hung out at the used record shop and thrift stores and would go home with great bargains, feeling very proud of myself.

We never went on a sleep over vacation but had a few day trips to the beach, and sometimes went to the drive-in. Six dollars a car load for two movies. Not bad for a whole family.

And clothes? I remember whining because I wanted a pair of Jordache jeans when I was in the middle school. Everyone had them but they were ridiculously expensive. When somehow my parents got them I felt like the richest kid in the world. One year we saw Izod alligator patches at the flea market. I was so excited. If my mom bought those and sewed them to my cheap sweaters no one would know. She sewed one on a little high. I recall going to school and not realizing until someone told me, that my alligator was almost up on my shoulder. I fought with whomever it was that it wasn't a fake Izod. But it was.

There were downsides to this idyllic existence. Worrying the rent wouldn't be paid. Not having a house like all my friends. Being hungry sometimes. We didn't starve but there wasn't a glut of food around like now. We had old cars that sometimes didn't run. For a while we didn't have a car at all, but there was a bus and I could walk anywhere I needed to go.

The shame and longing I sometimes felt instilled in me a drive to not end up like that. I wanted to do whatever possible so my future children would have everything. So I did what a lot of people do. I got a house I couldn't afford and took trips and bought my daughter all the name brand shoes and clothes and toys she wanted. I got myself in debt. A lot of it. I'm still working out of that. Would I do it again to save her the embarrassment of being "a poor kid?" Probably, but to a lesser extent.

But there were also times in my adult life when I wasn't living beyond my means.

When I got out of high school and got my own place, I went to college nights and worked two jobs. My apartment was tiny and I lived on Ramen Noodles. When I met Ivy's dad, on Fridays we'd get a large pizza for six dollars. That was our big night out. When we bought a house later, he and Ivy, a toddler then, built a stone wall outside made from slate he picked up over time in the woods or the side of the road. I made crafts for people to give as Christmas gifts because we didn't have any money.

I once bought a VW Bug for a hundred dollars. It never passed inspection but it was a memory. All our cars were from auctions and that was okay. It was hard time but it was real. When we split up, Ivy and I were pretty broke and when they gave food away after office lunches, those often became our dinner. We ate out sometimes but it was from the dollar menu or we'd split meals or drinks. I held it together for us and it was…memorable. Me and Ivy against the world; holding our little family together and taking pleasure in the small things.

When I married Husband #2, it was different. We turned my cute fixer upper into a show place. He owned nice cars. We took extravagant trips all over the world. Yes the culture was good for Ivy and me but there was never that sweetness, that special connection and excitement over bargains, or stretching a chicken to last a week, that came before. When we split up, I became stuck in material-things mode, bought what we wanted, took trips. Hence the debt.

Now Ryan and I are living in a cute rental house that we toy with buying. This year, 2016, I decided to become insanely frugal to save a down payment. With this process I was suddenly reminded how refreshing it feels to not spend money. To work with coupons and store hop and visit thrift stores on the last Saturday of the month to get fifty percent off. Getting a vintage painting for three dollars is exciting. Buying a week's groceries and vowing that that is what we are eating, reminds me of those old times. I regret forgetting where I came from because it was a place where working for what you had and appreciating it all was the norm. It was better.

I realize now that you can make pretty good money and still be frugal, still revel in the feeling of remembering what you really need and forgoing the impulse stuff. When you strip away the thousands of dollars of wasted spending, or clicking on every Amazon ad that looks appealing, when Buy-it-now become a taboo not a habit…it's pretty cool. It's freeing.

There seems to be a stigma in being frugal when you don't have to be, that is similar to being poor. People question you, look down at you when you don't want to go out to expensive dinners or on trips. When you decide to buy most of what you need at thrift stores. When you buy cheaper bulk meat in the smaller ethnic grocery stores and refuse, again and again, to buy the luxuries. Yes, there is a marked difference between needing to do this and wanting to, but it's brought back a long-lost feeling of peace, of earning and working for everything I buy.

That victory is lost when you just buy everything you want with no patience, no waiting, charging it all and losing track of what matters.

Family matters. Working hard and following dreams matters. Saving for your future and building financial security matters. Spirituality, religious or otherwise, matters. Thousands of dollars in Amazon purchases and restaurant tabs? Not so much.

Here's to a happy, frugal, and proud 2016. There's no shame in simplicity.

Adult Children, The Calm After The Storm

June 1, 2017

It's been well over a year since I blogged here, and figured I'd check in. Ryan and I bought the house we were renting, so the frugality worked wonders. We then spent the last year pouring money into it to fix all the things that made it so "cheap" to start with. Cheap is a relative term as this is southern California. But it was what we could afford and we feel like we got a steal. The house is adorable and filled with wonderful finds from thrift and antique stores. We have a true "home" where we can settle down and live happily ever after.

Ryan is good too and it's hard to believe it's been almost six years since we started "talking." But that's all a status update and laundry list, to catch everyone up.

The biggest thing that has changed is that Ivy has suddenly grown up. It's odd, not talking to her every day. I've gotten so I'm not overcome with sadness when she doesn't call, and don't dwell on it. I can go a full three days of silence before I break down and text messages like, "You're okay right, not in a ditch?" And she will reply that she's fine which is her cue to send me a few texts or call to fill me in on whatever is going on with her which seems to be also relatively peaceful.

It's the end of her third year not living with me/us and it's taken me this long to finally be okay with it. I've always been proud of her for moving out, and have understood this is what happens, the natural occurrence of things. But I haven't liked it. I spent the better part of the last almost three years being worried for her.

I remember being in the hospital after she was born. She was swaddled, on the bed with me, just a day or two old. I had this horrible sad, sinking feeling that now that she was on the outside I couldn't protect her anymore. As a mother, sure, I would cling to her as much as I could while allowing her to breathe, but once they're out, and in this big world, it's daunting.

Ivy's first two years of college, I think it's fair to say, were difficult. She had some good moments, but there was so much angst for her, and for me who was like ET and feeling all her pain. Many a time I wanted to go to school, pick her up, and make her move home, where I could coddle and take care of her. She said no. I guess my first couple of years away from home were hard, in different ways. And maybe that was hard on my mother.

But it appears the worst has passed, and like me, she has gotten used to the sunshine and the chipper, chill attitude of the people here. She doesn't call me all the time to fix her problems. If she has them she fixes them herself, or works through them with her boyfriend. We've seen more of the two of them lately and it's odd to have two young adults over for a meal or a visit, and just catch up and say hello. I'll call her boyfriend Trevor since no one has their real names on this blog.

I don't think I've seen Ivy this animated and "herself" since she was in middle school. She seems emotionally lighter, not so bogged down by life.

I blame myself for that life heaviness, for staying with Husband #2 for too long and letting him damage our self-esteem. For dating Rebound guys, for being impulsive. I did the best I could as a mother, but I assume that if I'd provided a solid father role model, it may have avoided some of her pain. It certainly would have helped avoid some of mine.

Now that I have Ryan though, and am settled, and she has Trevor, and is settled, the world is finally calm and breezy and nice. Not crazy, manic, frenetic, like when I was in my twenties, but nice. Ivy will still have a lot to get through with finishing school, getting a job, and all the other adult milestones she will face, but she is well on her way and that makes me about as content as a fat dog in a barrel of beef jerky.

Signing off for now.

The Most Important Things

December 11, 2017

Here I am, apologizing again for not writing more often. Days and weeks fly by and once in a while I realize I haven't documented any of it. But I often feel there is nothing to say except "Things are good."

They are good. Ivy is plugging along at school, a little behind schedule but enjoying the experience. I am constantly proud of who she has become. She is still seeing Trevor, and Ryan and I like him very much.

I got a new job last May. Same company but new position, new department, new everything. It was scary but rejuvenating to start over. Everything was unfamiliar, as was this new life I moved into three years ago, but I love it! Changing my entire life to move cross country gave me the strength I needed to move to another role at work. But enough with the status report.

The last few days' happenings struck a chord in me and I feel compelled to share my thoughts.

Last week a fire broke out in Southern California. Then another, and another, and so on. I have always felt insulated and safe in my town, from crime, earthquakes, fires. I suppose most of us feel safe until something happens, then we become cautious/cynical, much like I was jaded about love when I started this blog.

I accused Ryan of overreacting that morning when he said I should rethink going into the office. Then he gestured toward the TV and video coverage of the hill beside the 405, my route, aflame, from the Sylmar Fire. I begrudgingly stayed home. That sight began to fuel my worry. Like thousands of others, I spent most of the day glued to nonstop news reports on the fires, concerned and sad for others but not worried for us. All the fires were a good twenty miles away. We had smoke clouds over the house but surely that didn't mean anything.

But then my friend who works for the fire department said (and news reports confirmed) that we would have 50-75 mph winds that night and the Rye Fire would head to our town. Ryan was not worried, as he said it would not hit our side of town. But watching live telecasts of houses in Ventura burning to the ground from the Thomas Fire, I did not believe him. I wanted to pack, to be ready for an evacuation. He accused me of overreacting.

The next morning as soon as he went to work, I packed four large bins and one cardboard box. It was sobering to think that I had to choose only a small amount of things to bring, knowing that may be all that was left of the life I knew and loved. It made me wonder what really mattered and what didn't.

I love my home, and all the quirky things in it: the treasures from thrift stores and antique shops, my Zuni Warrior, and old crank Silvertone phonograph, and countless little carvings and trinkets that have been acquired and whose presence has resulted in our home starting to look like a curio shop. But I stopped and admitted to myself that most everything in the house was newly acquired after I moved here. It was only the items from before that mattered. Everything else could be rebought, rediscovered.

Of the four large bins, two were filled with photo albums, one filled with legal docs that made me realize I didn't need that many years of tax returns, and a large bin filled with Ivy's school papers. When she was little I started saving all her important school assignments from kindergarten through twelfth grade: science and history projects, shadowboxes, terms papers, and some of her earliest scribbles.

The cardboard box held Ivy's things:

• The most important books from her room: the Mother Daughter Book club books from our group that ran from fourth grade through the girls' freshmen year. I could re-buy those but...it wouldn't be the same.

• Her Bunny Box with all her gold coins from Santa and the tooth fairy, and some two dollar bills.

• Her (used to be favorite) two dolls she said I could get rid of a few years before, the ones I saved anyway.

• Her drawer of clothing labels she collected with her stepsister when she was little.

• The silver cup her Godparents gave her for her Christening.

• The whole collection of yearly Cherished Teddy statues her grandmother gave her each of her young birthdays.

Looking at the boxes and bins stacked in front of the garage door, ready to be loaded into the truck as soon as we got the call, it hit me how fleeting material things are, and also how quickly one can adjust to and love a new home, a new job, a new life partner, a new dog.

In the end, Ryan was right. The winds didn't come, the fire never made it to our town. I unpacked everything, relieved but wiser. The life we have right now, where we live, the stuff we have, the jobs we have... we delude ourselves into thinking that it's permanent, that we can snapshot it and live the same day over and over and nothing will change and we could not bear it if anything did.

Looking at the boxes showed me that it's not true. We could always start again, even without the five bins if it came to it. I didn't go to the thrift store this week to see what treasures I could potentially find to make our house a home. Turns out it's not the stuff that makes it a home but the people, the pets, and the love.

Closing out 2017, A Different Carly.

The Simplicity of Gingerbread

December 20, 2017

Last week Ivy went to Massachusetts to visit family. She brought Trevor along as well. It was their first big trip away together, and his first time meeting her dad's side of the family.

I was worried for a lot of reasons. The main ones are obvious: it might be too cold, or snowy. They wouldn't have enough money, and they'd get stranded. She'd hurt herself. The last time she went back east she broke her foot in two places and I had to arrange doctor visits from 3000 miles away. My mother surely had the same concerns when I went to Jamaica at the same age, with Ivy's dad, Arnie. We made it home plenty safe and I had to trust that she would too.

The biggest worry I had about this trip was about her seeing, and Trevor meeting, Arnie. When I met Arnie G. he was twenty-five and I was twenty-one. He was a free spirit and quirky. Easy to get along with, utterly brilliant, and he had freckles which was a plus because I really wanted my someday child to have brilliance and freckles.

But things go wrong sometimes and despite my blueprints for a perfect life, and despite my planning and lists, and my shooting for the stars, he...fell apart, irretrievably. It happened a few times and to quote Humpty Dumpty, no one could put him back together again. Sometimes he was fine and sometimes not. And the good days got fewer. Then there were drugs. No one can be sure if the drugs were a cause or symptom, a self-medicating treatment gone awry.

As the holidays near, and Ryan asks me if I want to make a gingerbread house, I think of Arnie and our early days, in our twenties. He was always up for anything, made a sincere effort to do what I asked, including helping me build my Martha Stewart Gingerbread Mansion. I could never keep it simple. I was always thinking big. I had a plan for my career, our house, our someday child. Everything arranged in checkboxes and columns.

My gingerbread mansion collapsed. It was uneven and the sugar glass windows were too heavy. The royal icing didn't act like glue like the magazine promised. Later my married life also collapsed, maybe because I could not keep it simple. Understandably, I cannot control or fix someone's mental illness or addiction which Alanon drilled into my head. But it must have been hard for Arnie to have me be so… Carly-esque, always striving for another goal, another milestone. I was taking the "don't forget where you came from" advice and turning it on its head. I was certainly going to forget where I came from, come hell or high water, and everything was going to be different in my adult life.

So I don't make gingerbread houses at all because I can't do it well and don't want to fail and as people sometimes tell me, I cannot just relax and have fun for fun's sake. Admittedly I am not a fan of whimsy but am working on it.

Ivy and I have not seen Arnie since her high school graduation party. Physically he has changed dramatically from when we met, and now, when his muscular atrophy is so severe that he can't walk without a cane and his hands are curled in and mostly useless. He also has a new symptom where his face twitches all the time (causing agony, he says). In a perfect world, he would go to the doctor, and see specialists until they could straighten it all out, or at least make him more comfortable. But when you are a mostly homeless person, and you have addictions, and a record, and you struggle with mental illness, it's not a level playing field when it comes to healthcare.

We didn't see Arnie much throughout most of Ivy's childhood. He was usually "not up to snuff" to use a euphemism. He's had ups and downs. He's in a good state now, is sober, texts and calls a lot. Ivy, like me, does not hate people for behavior they regret, if they try to fix it.

So she met him in Boston. Since she was three years old, she has only seen him twice without me there. And only for an hour or so each time. I told Trevor he had to be the mom for me, keep an eye on things, pull her away if she was sad or he was "not up to snuff." But it was fine. She was sad because of his physical condition and the way he lives. But he was happy that day, and she was too. I have a nice picture of them together, in the snow outside the Statehouse. There is something so genuine about his expression, the joy and pride in his face, that it's both heartwarming and heartbreaking. Despite his circumstances, he is impossibly happy in the now. They are both the exact same people they were eighteen years ago in many ways. He is a proud father, and she, a loving little girl who cares only that he loves her. Beyond that, nothing matters.

After she got back to California and returned to Santa Barbara, once the smoke from the local fires finally eased up, she sent me a picture. She said "Trevor and I built a gingerbread house last night." It was beautiful in that it wasn't perfect. It was a happy, sloppy creation with gingerbread people outside it, their frosted smiles decorating the gingerbread yard. There is even a peace sign frosted onto the gingerbread driveway. Very Ivy-esque.

She is more grounded than me, is happy with right now. She does not (often) agonize over the future, or unrealistic goals she has set for herself or others. She doesn't expect perfection in herself or others.

I can learn something from this, about the contrasts between her and me. Perhaps my painful "what not to do" life lessons have had the intended effect.

Her gingerbread house is likely to stand until she eats it or tears it down. I am proud of it, and her, and am inspired to try again and make one myself, with palm trees made of icing, and a structure that is both strong and yet imperfect, like me.

The True Smallness Of Bullies

January 8, 2018

My old dog Sally was eight pounds when we got her. We carried her everywhere, zipped up in our jackets. Later when she was eighty pounds, she didn't grasp why she didn't fit in our jackets. She did not know that if she wanted to attack and kill us, she could have. She did not comprehend that we were no longer twenty times bigger than her.

Sometimes a man will take a sweet puppy, abuse him, and make him mean. And that adult dog can rip out the throat of another dog, or intruder, or anyone he pleases. But will he attack his owner? No, because he doesn't know that his owner is no longer twenty times bigger than he is. He's been conditioned to be powerless to his master.

This conditioning works the same way for humans. Let's say you're a child with a violent father that beats or belittles you. It takes a long time until you grow up, and look down to find a wiry little bully, as pathetic and harmless as a cartoon character. It takes years to build up courage because you've *gradually* grown from a small child to an adult and didn't realize he is no longer many times larger than you.

I was fortunate that nearly all the father figures in my life (bio dad, stepfather, grandfather) were even-tempered and loving. But there was this one guy my mother dated who does not get a name in this blog because he doesn't deserve one. He will just be Mean Guy. How did he breeze in and take over our lives? It's because of her father.

Back when my mother was very small and her father was comparatively very big, he was an abusive tyrant. Had he lived longer than his thirty-three years (she was eight) she probably would have grown to see that he was just a miserable little man. When you took away his "giant" adult size and the liquor that increased his bravado tenfold, he was a petty malcontent. But he died, and so in her mind he is, still to this day, a scary memory, ever present in his demeaning, cruel behavior.

After my stepfather left, when I was high school, Mom started dating Mean Guy. She brought him home to meet my brother and me. I didn't like him. She, however, had never felt so close to someone. She felt "home" with him. It's no surprise that early on, we saw that he drank a lot. He was abusive and cruel. He'd been in jail for the attempted murder of his first wife. I believe, "beat to death but came back to life" was the wording that kept it from being actual murder. Semantics.

My mother went to counseling and Alanon for a short time after my stepfather left and at the beginning of the Mean Guy relationship. The counselor told her she was "finishing the story," both from her short time with her father, and then with my bio dad who had been in Vietnam like Mean Guy. The difference was that my bio dad didn't routinely go crazy and try to kill people, and his day job wasn't beating people up for bookies, and he didn't wave around brass knuckles and hand guns to intimidate innocent teenagers. So the "story" was not really the same at all except that she had left my bio dad shortly after he returned from Vietnam, and maybe dating and loving this "poor lost soul" all these years later would balance the scales and give her closure.

Except it didn't. And for ten years she was stuck in the climax scenes of a bad Lifetime Network movie. I was stuck in it too but had not been conditioned to fear or give in to people like him. I hated him and stood my ground which resulted in a great deal of friction. I had the "if you touch me you'll go back to jail" card that I played quite often. I moved out at Year Three once I turned eighteen.

Mean Guy and Mom were evicted for noise on Year Ten and so she left him and got her own place. She has not dated since 1993 because she "Doesn't know how to pick men." Rather she does not know how to differentiate from memories of past experiences and the reality of whoever is in front of her, snarling and manipulating. Was it really her relationship with Mean Guy that she could not afford to fail at, or someone else from an unfinished tragic story she was too young to control? We all replay our life situations over and over until we realize that nothing changes if nothing changes. But there's got to be a limit on this loop of self-destruction.

How does all this relate to dogs and bullies? Some dogs are walking around, perfectly happy until they see a guy with a hat, or a newspaper, or who wears the cologne of someone who abused them. They suddenly feel powerless and terrified. They are again an eight pound puppy who has no choice but to cower and do what the master wants, even if it's not their master but merely someone who set off a trigger.

Dogs do not just walk out the door and say "I've had enough. I can get my own food. I can go to a shelter and they will take care of me until a nice master comes along and loves me and treats me right." Dogs don't do that and sadly a lot of people don't either.

I know too many humans who stay in bad situations year after year saying they are afraid to leave because there will be retaliation, or they will miss the happy life their partners keep telling them they have, unaware of one major detail: the tragic reality of their life.

But it doesn't have to be like that. At some point, you *can* stand tall, look down on your bully and pop his overblown ego like a balloon that will deflate and whither down to flaccid pink rubber.

PEOPLE ARE NOT DOGS. We have choices. We are not twenty times smaller than our partners, as they would have us believe. Words and meanness are all they have. If they had more than that, we would stay.

To all the people in emotionally or physically abusive relationships, just go. Take your stuff and walk away with your tail wagging, not between your legs. There are kind people out there and a better life; your current partner just doesn't want you to know it.

-As always, grateful to my Ryan for his perpetual kindness.

Outside Looking In

January 17, 2018

One of my biggest fears is losing my mind. This worry stems, I think, from the fact that my brain is always going in a hundred directions, that my imagination is a little too strong, and that there are constant weird parallels in my life that make me wonder, too often, if I'm living in a video game.

They say there are only so many fiction plots, and I add that beyond that only so many subplots. Assuming our lives are predestined, there are only so many different situations we can encounter over the course of our lives before they start to repeat or overlap. I've mentioned these before in this blog: the time the priest who married my first husband and me twenty years prior, magically appeared in my life the day after I sold my engagement ring from Husband # 2. Or when I met my ex-stepfather again after twenty-five years and upon walking toward him ran into Ivy's ex-stepfather.

My life is fraught with parallels and coincidences and I have come to accept them as messages from some metaphysical being or God saying, "I'm giving you some clues here, some hints that you're on the right path." Stuff like that makes me wonder if I'm going crazy, but more often than not I like it and think it makes me special, in a good way, not the lock-you-up-in-an-institution way.

The other night I went to a hair salon to take a few inches off my uncontrolled mop. I never can remember the names of the hairdressers there, except for Ling but Ling is always booked in advance, and I always show up on whim. A very young, skinny, blonde girl (I'll call her Lori) said she could take me. I told her what I wanted and she began to snip away.

We talked as she cut. I explained that I was from Massachusetts, met a guy online, etc. Lori listened intently and then said, "My mother did the same thing. She met a guy online but from the east coast. They had a long distance relationship and flew back and forth a lot too. They've been together a few years and he just proposed to her and now she's moving out to Pennsylvania." I asked her age and she said twenty-one. The same age as Ivy. Lori is also an only child.

For a moment I thought, what are the odds? A girl Ivy's age whose mother meets a guy online and moves to the opposite coast? It was clearly another one of these little notes from the universe. So I waited with bated breath to see how she felt about it. Not that this necessarily reflects what Ivy thinks but it's been my experience with coincidences that they are pretty spot on.

We talked about relationships and how, above all else, I'm content and relieved to have a permanent partner who is nice. To have a best friend, a companion. To live without my focus being on fixing a broken relationship, or getting over a man, or finding a new one. She nodded and said she is very happy that her mother has someone to spend her life with, to settle down with, so she won't have to worry about her.

Children should not have to worry about their parents. They should be able to watch them being responsible adults, leading by example. I regret that many of Ivy's lessons learned about relationships were from my "This is what not to do," teachings.

Ivy has not said much about my relationship with Ryan in the past six years. She was never one to pull punches about other men I dated, or married.

Some of her most poignant comments, about various people were: "It makes me sick to look at him, he's obnoxious, he's conceited, he's stupid, he's crazy, he's lying, he's mean, he argues about everything..." I could go on all day. With Ryan, she never said a word, which was odd. Maybe because she knew how much he meant to me. Maybe because at that point she was tired of her very valid complaints falling on deaf ears. Maybe because Ryan didn't deserve her venom and she has never been critical without reason.

Last year Ryan bravely asked her if she liked him, sort of joking, as we assume by now that she does. She said quite plainly, "All we ever wanted was someone who was nice to me and to my mom. You've been nice so yes, I like you." Simple words but it's the core of so many successful relationships, and the lack of it is the downfall of so many more.

The hairdresser explained that her parents used to fight all the time. There was no physical violence but so much anger and shouting. This reminded me of the time Ivy and her stepsister at the time, they were about nine and seven respectively, put notes all over the house saying "STOP YELLING!" I told the hairdresser about this and how nice it is now that there is no yelling. She said there is no yelling in her mother's new relationship either.

I wondered, what was the message here? What was the universe trying to tell me? Then she said it. "I want to find someone to settle down with and have that kind of relationship. Like she has now. A best friend, someone to love, to depend on. Someone nice." And there it was. The new relationship is the one she's using as an example of how things are supposed to be, not the failed marriage of her parents. This revelation made me realize that Ivy may be using my relationship with Ryan as her basis for how things should work, not all my ghosts of relationships past.

Ivy has learned from me, for better or worse, and hopefully I met Ryan in time for her to see that there is such a thing as a good match. When I see her with Trevor, placid and peaceful, I think we are all on the right path.

Here's to looking for signs in everyday occurrences.

On Building
A Dollhouse

January 24, 2018

Ryan bought me a dollhouse for Christmas. I never had one as a child, except for a folding vinyl one we got at a flea market. Though I liked that one very much at the time, it was not a *real* dollhouse. I always wanted a big wooden house that I could decorate with wallpaper and paint and tiny furniture. I never managed to get one, and when I had Ivy I vowed that she would have a grand dollhouse. For some reason, her childhood went by too fast and I never managed to get her one either. She says she was just as happy with her multi-level grand Barbie house with an elevator but to me that does not count.

So on Christmas I opened a real dollhouse and was thrilled. It was a kit with a lot of pieces but that made it all the more fun, right? Well, yes and no. It took a week before I had time to open the box and pour out the pieces, which seemed to multiply before my eyes. I had only a grainy picture on the box to guide me as to the final result, and some simple directions. Simple here means not that they made it simple for me to assemble but that the manufacturer simplified his process by putting everything in basic, poorly drawn sketches and covered all the instructions in about ten pages.

To say I was intimidated is an understatement. For one, I expected to snap it together, paint it, furnish it, and display it in record time. It took a whole day just to dry fit the base together because I didn't understand the picture and kept taking it apart and putting it back together, second guessing every step. On the third try, I gave up and Ryan came out and took it apart and put it back together the exact same way and said the instructions were not confusing at all. But they were. I then watched YouTube Videos and read blogs about dollhouses. Most say you should paint the pieces first.

For a bit I sat, stunned, realizing that before I could build this I had to decide on colors, buy the paint and supplies, dry fit everything to make sure I had the right pieces in the right places, paint them, then glue them. With a lot of waiting in between. This would take forever!

Then I took a mental step back. So it takes forever. The point of the house, I understood then, was not to have something to display, but something to do, to experience. When the next weekend rolled around, I had my supplies, plenty of time, and a different attitude. All day Sunday, I painstakingly painted all the window frames on the first floor. I stained and polyurethaned the grand front door and porch railings. I thought ahead to paint the second floor piece white on one side for ceilings. I felt very clever and excited about my newfound dollhouse skills.

Then I started gluing. I forced a little window in and the wall itself got loose. Okay, I should have put the windows in before I put the walls up. Check. Lesson learned.

I glued all the window frames in and taped them up to hold them until the glue dried. I glued the front door in. I glued in the porch railings. And a few minutes later I realized the back of the railings were unstained. It was too late to take it all apart so I used a Q-tip dipped in stain and mostly covered everything.

Wow the first floor looked great, I thought. And I was thoroughly enjoying the process, learning what to do and what not to do. Like life, it's about the experience. It's about not making the same mistakes. I am sure that by the time I'm working on the top floor I will have this all figured out and hopefully no one will notice the errors on the first two floors.

With life, I am hoping people just focus on the NOW me, on my NOW life, not all the foolish, inept things I did when I was younger and just learning.

I looked at the grainy sketch of the house from the outside of the box. Life is very much like building a dollhouse. You see a picture of a grandparent or distant relative, someone the family speaks of with reverence. You wonder how she got to be like that, how to achieve what she did. There are no good instructions, just the bare bones you may hear about. She worked hard, got a degree, got married...

No one supplies the details of how she became successful. How she became an incredible matriarch that everyone looked up to. I am sure that if you were to see the details of such a life, you would find mistakes she made along the way. But we only look at the finished product. We remember the final person, and tend not to dwell on what she was before, unless we are resentful and hateful people (which I am not).

When I went to take pictures of my house in progress I was miffed to discover that my forgetting to paint the backsides of the window frames mattered. From the inside, they were unpainted and wood burned in some areas. It was too late to start over. I hadn't thought about the inside of the house. Alas, another metaphor for life. We do not think about the insides, what we assume people cannot see. We strive for the outside appearance. The paint and stain and what the structure looks like. We tend not to focus on how we feel, the guilt we have, the sacrifices we've made, the compromises, the triumphs. We focus on what people will see. And there is no starting over.

In the end my dollhouse will look beautiful, because of what I've learned, because of the time I spent, and the enjoyment and frustrations I poured into it. Because only I know the errors I made and how hard I worked to get things right, and how proud I was when I did get things right. To someone on the outside, it may look a little flawed. Perhaps I'll hang tiny wallpaper that isn't the right scale, or I'll use lavender paint in the living room that a miniature expert will think looks gaudy. But to me it will be just right, because at the end of the day I am supposed to make my own happiness. What others think should not penetrate the walls of this little house that is crafted with love and hope and dreams. This little house that symbolizes me, my struggles, and my pride in building a life.

Perhaps my foundation was shaky and I had subpar instructions, but in the end, I think me and my house will turn out just fine.

To building a life.

The Inner Judge

February 7, 2018

The other day I went into an upscale burger place in our town to set up a fundraiser for a pet rescue I'm involved with. While I waited for the manager, I saw two middle class, middle aged men walk up to the counter together to get their trays of food. One of the men grabbed a double burger from the tray and dashed outside. My instant reaction was that this guy was jerk. He didn't even say goodbye to his friend, just snatched the food and ran out. What an antisocial creep, I thought. I got a little angry and rolled my eyes.

Luckily, I kept an eye on the hamburger grabber and felt like a judgmental idiot when I saw him hand the burger to the bedraggled looking, probable homeless man outside. The scraggly man smiled and took the burger to go with drink he already had (surely the man bought that too). Then the middle aged man came back in, rejoined his friend, and they took the trays and went off to sit. I noticed as the man walked away that he wore an L.A. City Fire t-shirt. So he saves lives and gives food to homeless people. Good job, Carly, wrongly judging a really good guy based on…what exactly?

It got me wondering why we put labels on people. I talked to Ryan about it on the way home, how when you're younger you need labels so you can tell one person from another. Dangerous person, nice person, old person, child, parent, teacher, policeman, etc. We learn labels from parents and from society and it's important to know who people are so we can stay safe. But as we grow up, it goes one of two ways.

You cling to the identifying tags you learned through experience, and die with an unwavering conviction that all X types are bad and all Y types will hurt you, and you are the only one who is truly good and smart and worthy. I know too many people who slap labels on every poor soul who is not just like them. Are they so lacking in self-awareness that they truly think they are better than everyone? Or do they have so little confidence that they need to put others down to feel good? Whatever the causation, it makes for a lot of negativity inside them and to the ones who endure their judgment.

The second way it can go is that you grow up. You learn lessons from those around you who are different. You put yourself in their shoes, and you understand.

When I was younger, I was pretty self-righteous. Maybe I didn't come right out and say, "I would NEVER do that. I can't believe you live your life that way." But I thought it. A lot. Maybe I said it too. I hope not. But time humbles a person; and over the years I took on a lot of roles I may have turned my nose up at before. I've been divorced twice, lived with men out of wedlock, didn't finish college, drank enough alcohol to throw up a bunch of times, got a tattoo, declared bankruptcy, gave away a dog I couldn't control, smoked cigarettes, raised my daughter on takeout food...the list goes on and on.

All things my younger, perfect-self vowed never to do.

But as you live life, you often start becoming all the things you rallied against. It takes the wind out of your sails in a hurry, and you gain compassion because you know how it feels to be on other side. I've lived in some very low rent apartments and some fancy houses. I've been a registered Democrat, Republican, and have voted third party. I did the Atkins diet and ate mostly meat for a year. And now I'm a tree hugging vegetarian in Southern California. I never saw that happening. The California part at least. I think I always had an inner hippie.

And for everything I wasn't: homeless, a minority, chronically ill, elderly, fiercely religious, gay, a drug addict or alcoholic, violent, mentally challenged, very rich, college educated, depressed, schizo-phrenic... I have been very close to people who are those things and it gave me perspective.

I consider myself a self-aware, kind person. But then there was the guy the other day. The inner me burst out, unfairly labeling and judging the kind man who was bringing food to a homeless guy, reminding me that old habits die hard. I wanted to smack my smug inner voice.

Inside, we are all just humans, crossing paths on this planet at the same time. We have different journeys but share the same roads. And it's a much better experience if you learn to respect your fellow travelers and see them as they are, not through the lenses of your own biases.

It's good that once in a while I am reminded that I'm not quite there yet and still have a lot of work left to do.

Here's to true kindness.

Fountain Of Youth

February 27, 2018

When you're a kid, your life revolves around playing with your friends and focusing on the *now*. You give very little thought about the future because the assumption is that you will live forever. You haven't yet learned about race or class, or that you are better than or less than a friend because of social standing. It's a time of purity and wonder.

As you age you measure yourself against others, obsess about achieving. You feel inadequate if your house isn't big enough, or if you can't afford a house. If you have a job you love it's not good enough; you need to get a higher position in the company to feel validated, and make more money for a bigger house. These are generalizations. There are plenty of people who live frugally and have the home and car they need and do not spend their lives discontented with their present station in life. Good for them. They are a step ahead of the rest of us for whom there is a burning desire to fare better than our parents did, live in a nicer place, get more education...

A couple of weeks ago, Ivy and I took an unexpected trip to the Salton Sea, to visit my father and step mother, Lola. It's about a two hundred mile drive to their place, which we'd never seen. When I've visited them in the past bunch of years, it was at my sister Tammy's place in Arizona. Ivy hadn't seen them since she was nine years old which was way too long.

Ivy and I drove, chatting along the way as the miles flew past. As we neared the destination, there was a movie-like fade in. Windmills. Hundreds and hundreds of them in sync, blowing, spinning round and round like enormous pinwheels. I imagined a voice narrating the beginning of the adventure: "And now it begins..."

After the surreal windmill scene, miles and miles of nothingness followed. Dry, dead, drought grass as far as we could see.

Then suddenly to our right we saw light gleaming off the Salton Sea, the one-time tourist attraction extraordinaire turned highly salinated, somewhat toxic, dead-fish-on-its-shores site. It's stunning to see, as mesmerizing as any real ocean, with its sparking waters, and rhythmic waves. It was a joy to spot this oasis, this vast rolling ocean in the center of miles of barren landscape.

Before long we saw the mobile home park up on the left, a bright white oval eye against a flat, dry yellow face. I know, I know, me and my symbolism. In my defense, the park is called Fountain of Youth so I'm not the only one who is a symbol enthusiast.

This 55+ park is where Dad and Lola have spent most of their time in the last nine years or so, going up north to another park in summers, or to stay with Tammy. Once we passed through the security gate, Lola pulled up on a golf cart and told us to follow her. We drove down the small cozy paved roads, peppered with flowering shrubs and trees, until we reached their home. We dropped off our things, jumped in the cart, and drove to their friend Sophie's lot where we spent most of the rest of our visit.

There was a parade that day, and we watched as the residents, all of them good friends, marched on with their floats, each proudly showing off their activity: hiking, bocce, golf. People from all around the world ended up there. Two fire trucks showed up for the parade too and everyone waved at them. Lola said they see the emergency workers a lot because it's a senior park and people are always dying. She said it as a matter of fact, no emotion or commentary. I thought of a neighborhood of children, when suddenly one child leaves in a moving truck, never to be seen again. You move on and just enjoy the friends you have left. The residents here do the same.

After the parade, the crowd flowed up to the deck at Sophie's place, the roomy home with the desert and sea view, with a wall of bright pink azaleas and a mini Mourning dove who watched us suspiciously from her nest. The Chocolate Mountains perfectly completed the backdrop. The whole day felt like a movie broken up into scenes with Ivy and I moving from seat to seat, spending time with different combinations of Dad and Lola and their friends, listening to their conversations, telling them our stories.

There was a lot of champagne flowing that day, and the people at the party were as lively as college students, and enjoying their lives just as much. Fountain of Youth, indeed. From what I saw and heard, their days consist of hanging out and playing, reading, enjoying the pool and hot tub, and taking walks with their dogs. Their pensions or social security or savings cover their expenses. They can just enjoy living, having earned it after so many years of "adulting." I'm sure there are real issues they deal with beneath the surface, worrying about their grown children, or people they have conflicts with, or their health; but for the most part, they collectively seemed to be content to *be*, just where they landed.

At one point I sat with a British man from Canterbury. He and I sat on a wicker couch. I asked him what he did...before. Everyone here was retired after all, and from all over the world. I was curious about his job when he was on the work force. He paused, said no one ever asked that. He was fine with telling me but realized no one ever asked. His life before does not matter for this blog, only the point that everyone in the park lives in the *now*. He looked around and pointed, "I don't know what *he* did before, or *him*, or *her*..." but added, "They're good people."

I suggested that everyone was on a level playing field here, it seemed. He said yes, exactly. Some of them had a lot of money, some not so much. In the complex, there were probably doctors and lawyers and who knows what, but now they were retired and what they had before or were before...none of that mattered here. He said something along the lines of, "I'll probably die here but I'm okay with that. I like it here."

It got me thinking. At the end of the day, or the end of your life, when careers are over and your children are grown with children or grandchildren of their own, it's *your* time. Your season to hang out with friends, and relax, and talk about the journey you are on together, in the *now*. Because *then* is long gone and what remains is all that matters. All the corporate climbing, and the fancy cars and clothes, and how popular you were in high school, it matters so little in the scheme of things.

Now they are all living in similar small seasonal homes, drinking champagne on a deck, and looking over at an ocean that was at its prime when they were children. And like them, time may have changed it, weathered it, made it not as healthy as it once was; but it is just as strong and vibrant and full of life.

They take each moment for what it is. One bocce tournament at a time, one karaoke night, one homecoming parade, one round of golf on the sand course, one friend leaving forever in an ambulance...

The next morning we went to Bombay Beach before breakfast. To me it was a sad, forgotten place. The area was mostly abandoned. The beach sported derelict buildings and structures that many years ago could have been thriving hot dog stands or amusement park rides. I pictured tourist families running around on the beach, excited to be escaping from their life to come to this miracle ocean. I contrasted it to life *now*: the empty beach, the empty buildings. No one around except for some residents who live close by, in the tiny area of homes before the vastness that stretches on until the park where Dad and Lola live.

We went to the American Legion and met their friends from the night before. A man who was probably eighty held up a paper cup with a Bloody Mary in it—the drink of choice for all of them. "Some party last night!" I didn't know him but laughed at the relaxed frivolity amongst them. In the corner, an older man played his guitar and sang country music. We sat with Dad and his friends at a long folding table, and we ordered off a paper slip menu with check boxes. It was an adventure.

I couldn't help but imagine the narrator's voice then, the Buddha-esque Carly who puts things in perspective. "This is the scene where you look around and drink everything in. Where you came from, where they came from does not matter. You are part of their journey and they are part of yours." Their friend Sophie looked at me then and smiled. "There's a lot of kindness here." Her eyes scanned the room as mine did. "A lot of kind people."

A short while later, Ivy and I said our goodbyes and began the drive alongside the Salton Sea, now to our left. We drove until we were surrounded by the windmills again, lulling us back from what felt like our dream sequence, the symbolic end of our trip. And into the heavy traffic of the 10 and the 5 and the 118…and back to our own version of *now*. The hurried, break-neck pace of our lives with jobs and college and our everyday challenges.

There is something to be said for retirement, and slowing down, and appreciating life at face value, seeing your friends as you did when you were children, without the filters of color or finances. The gift is to savor what is here now and not what is next. Life is fleeting, and the next thing may never come. But *now* is all around us, and there is a lot of kindness here.

And that is what I learned on my trip to see my father.

White Noise

April 4, 2018

A couple of years ago, I bought a white noise machine for the bedroom. I'd heard about them for years but never saw the point. I like to sleep with quiet, not noise. Ivy's dad bought one years and years ago, before Ivy was born. It wasn't white noise though, it was rain and forest sounds. That was fine but then there would be a random cricket or a bang of thunder and I'd pop awake.

But I bought this machine anyway, probably on a Black Friday sale or something, I don't recall. What I do recall is that by about day three, I couldn't sleep without it. It shut out all the other real life noises, like dogs and cats jumping off the bed, or Sugar Glider barks, or crickets in the bathroom, or neighbors driving by. And mostly, it quieted the noises in my head.

I won't go so far as to say there are voices in my head, because that sounds too much like insanity. But there is a lot of noise all the time, a lot of my own thoughts, and replays of songs, or television shows, or general music, plus the sound memories of a million different experiences from the day going a thousand miles an hour. There are endless what-if scenarios running on all the time, being played out layer after layer. Sometimes the white noise machine isn't enough but it certainly takes the edge off.

I bring this all up because about a month ago I decided I needed to give up added sugar. My weight has gone up and down a bunch of times since I started this blog. I'm on an upswing now. I'm pretty heavy but holding fast and not gaining. I gave up eating meat about six months ago and gained weight because I was eating a lot more carbs. I'm sticking to being a vegetarian but there's no excuse for all the sugar. Plus, as I age my cholesterol is going up. I'd never read labels for sugar before and certainly never really thought of it as anything but my harmless and much-adored drug of choice.

The first few days of not having sugar were miserable. I was shaky and so hyper even I wanted to slap me. Seeing the effects of withdrawal sort of woke me up to how addicted I truly was. After that initial adverse reaction though, I became calm. Too calm. The noise in my head was gone. It was uncomfortable for me, this silence. There was just...nothing. I felt depressed, which is not like me.

As moods go, I'm mostly zippy and bubbly all the time. I've been likened to Winnie the Pooh, Pollyanna, and Holly Hunter's role in *Broadcast News*. But suddenly I was flat and sad. I took some vacation time from work to use up days and binge watched TV. I didn't write at the same time or work on my dollhouse or read. I just sat. I was worried I was actually "depressed" and not just blue. Then I became concerned that maybe this was the new normal. Maybe this is how regular felt and I was usually so (sugar) high all the time I didn't know it.

I craved the erratic chaos in my head, the wide-awakedness, the creativity I couldn't staunch. But it was just white noise inside. I had physical energy. Too much really, so I was still jazzed up that way. I did a ton of yard work and carried 130 bags of mulch, some in the rain, to spread. I laid weed barrier and hurt everything in my body. I weeded the hill and sliced my dirt-packed finger on a palm tree and kept working. But the frenetic mental self, the crazy Carly inside, she wasn't there.

I met a guy in an airport once who asked if I was Hypo Manic. I said no. He said he was and he took meds for it and it changed his life. He explained that most people hover a little above and a little below the normal mood range. And people like us, we're almost always up up up. It's not as drastic as bipolar. It's like mini bipolar. But without as much down. At least that's how I understand it. Back then I questioned why the heck I'd want to tamp down my constant happiness.

But after the last few weeks I kind of get it now. Part of me was sad because I missed the high, the explosion of mental positive energy and creativity that NEVER SHUTS DOWN. And the other half of me was so damn relieved to rest. To shut down and stare at the TV and binge watch Netflix shows. That side of me dreaded when the next wave of super energy would come back because I realized then how utterly exhausting that can be.

It's been a month since I gave up added sugar, or at least knocked it way down. I feel okay now, not sad, not excited just kind of even. I still get a little burst of happiness from hugging Ryan or the pets, or looking at the flowers in my garden, but I'm not Roger Rabbit happy, and that's okay.

Maybe as time goes on my brain will continue to readjust to the lack of sugar, and will rewire. I will be super hyper all on my own, driving everyone around me to drink. Or maybe the little white noise machine in my head will keep running, and I will know how it is to feel quiet, to feel placid.

This is my first blog in a month or so and I guess that says something about my emergence from the "drug" withdrawal. I made it through Easter without Cadbury Eggs which is a feat all on its own. Today I picked up a Snickers three times in the store and set it down. I then picked up a Three Musketeers. I set that down too and left with fresh strawberries.

I'm not saying sugar has shaped my personality, only allowed it to flourish and go unchecked and unbridled. Maybe I won't be writing a book a year, and writing screenplays and stories and trying to learn Spanish and renovating the house and volunteering and working full time...but I'm good with that.

For the first time in my life, I think I'd be good to just sit for a while and be content and hear...nothing.

To accepting tranquility.

Learning From The Young

May 1, 2018

Until I was old enough to attend kindergarten, all my knowledge came from my stay-at-home mother. The way I talked (wicked strong New England accent), the truths: wear clean underwear in case you have a car accident, always use mayonnaise and never Miracle Whip, spicy things will hurt your stomach, grease and flour your cake pans, color in the lines, connect the dots in order, the world is scary, new things are scary. My mother's view was my view of the whole world.

By middle school though, and certainly by high school, I formed my own opinions. And in my teen years I went through a phase where I fought vehemently that all her ideas were wrong and all mine were right. I lacked the perspective of aging and failing at my endeavors, so for that short time I was utterly brilliant.

When I was a teenager, I did a lot of babysitting. Two of my wards were adorable British children with even more adorable accents. I asked my mother at the time why they had accents if they were born here. She explained to me that they spent almost all their time with their British mother, but once they went to school and were exposed to American children, they would assimilate and lose their charming way of speaking. Years later, my mother ran into the family and confirmed that they were 100% Americanized.

I thought of this recently and how many parts of me changed

from when I was a child, once I assimilated to all the people outside my home. The kicker is that a lot of the internal stuff is still there. So many of the major decisions in my life were made by the sheltered child inside, the one who still has the accent, who doesn't color outside the lines. We may learn to talk differently, to dress differently, but aren't our strictest convictions and beliefs the ones from our childhood: fear of dogs, and mean men, and monsters in the closet, of being left? We don't easily let those things go.

My mother knew, and told me, everything about her past and the past of the world she grew up in, from *her* perspective. I took her past, and my present and future and ran with it. I relayed to her what I found, what I discovered along the way, things that were different from what she'd understood to be true. I tried to tear away the beliefs she'd had since she was that sheltered child. Similarly, in the last few years, as Ivy has grown into a young woman, I have learned from her. Be it new speech or new food or habits, in many ways, she has become my guide.

We moved to California a few years ago, and she became a vegetarian. Without planning to, so did I. I can talk to her about relationships and friendships and she gives good advice, better than I would have given at that age. I don't know when she became so sage, but I sense a reversal of the teaching process.

As with my mother, I can teach Ivy everything about my past, and the past of the world I grew up in, but I know so little about the present, how things are now outside of my bubble and my experiences.

When I was young, I spent so much time growing and learning about who I wanted to be. As we age, we become formed and solid. That quest to change and develop slows down. It is our children, or any younger people we know, who pull us along to remind us that we are *not* done growing and changing. Until we are dead, we have life lessons to learn.

Ivy brought up a good point the other day, that she heard somewhere. If someone bangs into you walking on a sidewalk, you determine immediately that the person was not paying attention and is a jerk. But if you then discover that person is blind, you will grasp that your take on the situation was skewed. You will reconsider and feel like a heel.

We have run ins with people all the time, on social media, at work, on the freeway, and we are quick to get angry. But we should apply the same kindness and understanding we felt running into a blind person (blind being a metaphor for someone whose condition is not what we think). Everyone who irks us is not *blind*, but they may have something going on that we do not understand. Great advice from my teacher, Ivy, and another lesson to add to those that guide me on my path.

Many people resist new ideas, new perspectives. They feel they have earned the right to sit back and cruise for a bit, with the knowledge they accumulated over a lifetime. But knowledge is a relative term based largely on truths drilled into our heads as children, or personal experiences from a set point in time, with a set cast of characters. We can ruminate over our pasts all we want, and rehash all that happened, but in the end, it's only new perspective that changes our minds, and then only if we are willing to accept it.

I do not want to be bound to the past, and use only that as a reference for pivotal life decisions or for how I treat people. You can learn a lot from your elders, but you can learn much from your children too.

I may have lost my New England accent (for the most part) but so much of me is still that child inside, watching and listening for perspective, growing and developing into who I am going to be.

In the words of Ivy,

Peace Out

The Heart Grows Fonder

May 11, 2018

I drove Ryan to the airport early Wednesday morning so he could visit his father in Minnesota. We're together almost all of the time but I rarely mention him in this blog anymore except as "Ryan said this" or "Ryan commented that…" It may seem that the big love affair I captured in the blog over six years ago has lost its magic. It has not.

After spending only two nights alone, it has hit me how close we are. I don't mention him just as I don't mention that I have curly hair, or a penchant for being hypersensitive, or that I have big feet. These are all part of what makes me the person I am. It's not that Ryan formed me into someone else; he's fostered my Carly-ness from day one. But he is always by my side in a way I hadn't realized until this week when suddenly he wasn't.

I glance fondly around the quiet house we share, our old Granville House, named from *It's a Wonderful Life*. We called the house this initially because it's on a street with the same name as the one from the movie—a fact my aunt pointed out before we moved in. Like the derelict Victorian in the film, our home was long empty, beaten down and worn, and in need of someone to bring it back to life. I had a sign made for the outside that proudly proclaims it as Granville House, because we are corny and romantic that way.

After we moved in, a Carly-esque coincidence happened. On

looking through some old documents from the original owner, I got a big surprise. The previous owner was a widow who lost her husband and son many years before, and who herself had passed away about four years earlier. The legal document I found listed the widow's late husband's first name: Granville. We were shocked by this, as we'd been calling it Granville House the whole time meaning something else entirely. Truly it was Granville's house. Signs like this cemented the fact that we were on the right life path.

The last couple of days I've worked eight hours (from the living room/my home office) then spent long, quiet, lonely evenings missing Ryan. I have my animals as companions. Rebound Dog Lily is almost seven years old now. Hard to believe it was that long ago I crept into a Starbucks to write a blog about dating and how I was never going to do it again. About how I was going to get a rebound dog instead. My full-blood, nine-hundred dollar Yorkie ended up being a mixed breed (so says her DNA). She weighs fifteen pounds, is deaf, has two leaky heart valves and a murmur. She's had 19 teeth removed this year and has no enamel on the others so will lose those at some point too. But she's the sweetest dog I've ever had. The absolutes I proclaimed about dog breeds, and my chronic checklists about everything—that's not me anymore.

A couple of years ago Ryan and I went to the pet store to get Henry (my now nineteen year old cat) some food. We spotted the pen of rescue dogs in the main aisle and fell in love with Scruffy. Ryan was resistant to adopt at first, until the little ragamuffin looked in his eyes. A ten month old they found in the street, the lady said, saved from a kill shelter. It's funny how close Lily and Scruffy have become. They're inseparable in the way Ryan and I are. They may not be glued to each other 24/7 but you can be sure that if one of them goes somewhere without the other (like the vet) there is panic. Like me, Lily was resistant at first to the idea of someone new in her life. She spent two solid weeks running away from Scruffy, avoiding eye contact if I held her up to the new dog, much the same way I avoided even the concept of having a new relationship. Then one day, she realized that Scruffy was the best thing that ever happened to her.

I love my house, filled with the touches that make it a *CarlyRyan* museum of sorts. Little bits of things collected since we met online. From the jar of rain I sent him from Massachusetts so many years ago, to the old Coke machine we got at the thrift store in our town. Everything in the home speaks of "us." There was never the conflict of my stuff/your stuff I've had in other relationships. Sure, he's got his book room, and the hall closet that's a book nook, and I've got my Harmony Box collection and some dolls, but the feeling when you enter Granville House is one of peace, contentment, and unity.

Ivy is graduating next week from her community college. She's a couple of years behind my original plan, but schedules, like lists, have become insignificant to me. Living and enjoying life is what matters. She started her new job this week, working with autistic children and adults. She will work there full time in the summer and hopefully part time in the fall. In August she will start school full time at a California state school to finish those final two years toward her bachelor's degree. I have never seen her so happy and relaxed and content with life. I have never seen myself that way, until now. The path we're on certainly seems to be the right one. It's where we belong. Neither of us would be here, if not for Ryan.

In the early days of my relationship with Ryan, when we only emailed each other, when we had no idea our casual correspondence would turn into a cross-country, long-distance romance, he sent one message that will always stick with me. I've quoted this before but it was early on and bears repeating. *"You've had a bad run of luck and you are a bit punch drunk. This is going to change for you..."*

He was certainly right about that.

I sit now in the living room, looking out the French doors to the patio, where my plants and flowers thrive. Greens and pinks and yellows and reds blend together like a kaleidoscope. Lily and Scruffy snuggle together in a basket. They are as bonded and as close as two beings can be while still retaining their individual personalities.

I look wistfully over at the side of the couch where Ryan normally sits. We watch television at night, continually pausing the show to discuss things. He'll hand me his phone and say "Hey did you see this story about it..." Or I'll stop the movie to read him a text Ivy just sent. Or we put her on speaker when she calls and we lean into the phone to hear about her day. He generally falls asleep during whatever show we turn on. And he's up long before me, in his study, doing book layouts. He's quiet and unobtrusive, but his presence is inexorably linked to mine. He is my best friend, and he is my home.

His absence is tangible right now, but thankfully he will be home in two days, back to me, his dogs, his old cat, his older turtle, and our happy little life in the old Granville House.

Here's to love.

TRACY L. CARBONE

Tracy L. Carbone is the author of six novels and two short story collections. She is the editor of the Bram Stoker Award nominated anthology *Epitaphs: A Journal of the New England Horror Writers,* and co-editor of *Cemetery Riots: A Collection of Dark Cautionary Tales.* A lifelong resident of New England, Tracy now lives and writes in the sunshine and warmth of Southern California.

SHADOWRIDGE PRESS

shadowridgepress.com

www.ingramcontent.com/pod-product-compliance
Lightning Source LLC
LaVergne TN
LVHW011321080426
835513LV00006B/144